The Usual Suspects
Staff

Editor R. V. Branham

Office Mgr. Sofia Sensei Satori Shostakovna Satyagraha Stolicniya Sashimi Shitkicker

Assoc. Editor T. Warburton y Bajo

Contrib. Editors T. Warburton y Bajo & Channing Dodson & M. F. McAuliffe & Michael Lohr & Douglas Spangle

Field Correspondent Michael Lohr

House Tr. T. Warburton y Bajo (Sp.), Miguel Caminhão (Portuguese), チャニング・ドッドソン (Japanese). Алекса Сигала & Андрей Сен-Сеньков (Russian), Ani Gjika (Albanian), Anggo Genorga (Tagalog), Michael Lohr (Scand.) & rvb (Sp., & select Eng.), & a cohort of Croatian & Lithuanian translators

House Spanish Copyediting Lyda Alvarez, M.F. McAuliffe

Cover Illo Graham K. Willoughby *Design* T. Warburton y Bajo

Cover comix & phfoto illos & franking Knut van Brijs & var Postal Services.

Photos (except as noted) M. F. McAuliffe, T. Warburton y Bajo

BCN Photos Sergio Morera, Marc Cristany & Laura Lobera

Layout T. Warburton y Bajo & R. V. Branham

Prod. Tools InDesign, Photoshop (occasionally, when functional), Gimp, Dreamscope

Tech Support Sam Ward

Additional Editorial & Design Asstance Douglas Spangle & M.F. McAuliffe

Legal Peter Shaver

Publisher GobQ LLC/Reprobate Books

Double Trouble Flipbook double Issues printed Nov. & May of ea. year.

Post-production printing Ingram Spark/Lightning Source

Also distrib. & printed nationally & internationally through Ingram Spark/Lightning Source POD

Sold through independent bookstores & available through Ingram & amazon dot com & WWW dot GobshiteQuarterly dot com

P.R. P. H. Vazak

Gobshite Quarterly: Double Trouble, Nos. 29/30, Winter & Spring 2018

ISBN 978-1-63587-868-4

GobQ volunteers: Qualified candidates please send résumé to

GobQ. LLC, 338 NE Roth St., Portland, OR 97211, or to gobq@yahoo.com

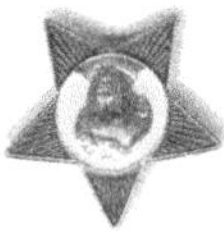

Gobshite Quarterly

Double Trouble / Issue 29 – Winter 2018

12.00 USDOL | | € 8.03462 EURO | | £ 6.36 GBP (UK) | | $ 12.0281 AUD (Oz) | | $11.4795 CAN | | ¥ 1,179.53 JPY (japan yen) | | 115.380 SAR (S. Africa)

This issue is dedicated to the memory of:

Olive Yang (楊金秀) a.k.a., Yáng Jīnxiù; Miss Hairy Legs (24 June, 1927 — 13 July, 2017)
Martin Landau (20 June, 1928 — 15 July, 2017)
John Heard (7 Mar., 1946 — 21 July, 2017)
Sam Shepard (5 Nov., 1943 — 27 July, 2017)
Brian Aldiss (18 Aug., 1925 — 19 Aug., 2017)
Dick Gregory (12 Oct., 1932 — 19 Aug., 2017)
John Abercrombie (16 Dec., 1944 — 22 Aug., 2017)
Jeannie Rousseau (1 Apr., 1919 — 23 Aug., 2017)
Mireille Darc (15 May, 1938 — 28 Aug., 2017)

Gobshite Quarterly

Double Trouble / Issue 30 – Spring 2018

This issue is dedicated to the memory of:

John Ashbery (28 July, 1927 — 3 Sept., 2017)
Holger Czukay (24 Mar., 1938 — 5 Sept., 2017)
Kate Millett (14 Sept., 1934 — 6 Sept., 2017)
Toshihiko Nakajima (中嶋 聡彦) (12 Aug., 1962 — 8 Sept., 2017)
J.P. Donleavy (23 Apr., 1926 — 11 Sept., 2017)
Sir Peter Hall (CBE) (22 Nov., 1930 — 11 Sept., 2017)
Grant Hart (18 Mar., 1961 — 13 Sept., 2017)
Harry Dean Stanton (14 July, 1926 — 15 Sept., 2017)
Kit Reed (7 June, 1932 — 24 Sept., 2017)
Danielle Darrieux (1 May, 1917 — 17 Oct., 2017)

12.00 USDOL | | € 8.03462 EURO | | £ 6.36 GBP (UK) | | $ 12.0281 AUD (Oz) | | $11.4795 CAN | | ¥ 1,179.53 JPY (japan yen) | | 115.380 SAR (S. Africa)

Gobshite Quarterly
Double Trouble / Issue 29 - Winter 2018

GobQ contributor Sergio Morera, Barcelona, 1 Oct., 2017:
Vote Schmote! ¡Vota Escamota!

L'Estat va dir "no hi haurà urnes", i va haver-hi.
L'Estat va dir "no hi haurà paperetes", i va haver-hi.
L'Estat va dir "no votareu", i vàrem votar.
L'Estat diu "no hi haurà canvi", i el canvi està arribant.

El Estado dijo "no habrán urnas", y las hubo.
El Estado dijo "no habrán papeletas", y las hubo.
El Estado dijo "no votaréis", y votamos.
El Estado dice "no habrá cambio", y el cambio está llegando.

The State said "there will be no urns", and there were.
The State said "there will be no ballots", and there were.
The State said "you will not vote", and we voted.
The State says "there will be no change", and the change is coming.

Respectfully flip the book over, as Issue 30, Spring 2018, is a whole upsy-daisy 62 pgs away fr. the Winter 2018 issue

Gob Words

A word to give offense, when offense may be due. ***Gobshite***, per OED, is what the American crew of Adm. Perry's Expedition to Japan were called by the natives; Amer. Heritage Dictionary, 4th. ed., refers to a wad of expectorated chaw *&* to the Old Eng. *Shiten*; yet another dictionary refers to a Gobshite as a "*pernicious blatherskite*"— i.e., a stiff to read the teleprompter feed for CNN or Rupert Murdoch's Fox "*News*" bullshit mtn. *&* those offended by the word can now be offended trilingually *&* quadrilingually, because all English-lang. pces have a foreign lang. *en-face* escort, whether Spanish, Arabic, Icelandic, Farsi, Albanian, Finnish, French, Portuguese, Italian, Russian, Lithuanian, Gaelic, Japanese, Korean, Tagalog, or whatever language is willing to put on its UN Observer cap. Wasn't it Pulitzer who said that journalism should comfort the afflicted *&* afflict the comfortable? Finally, a Rosetta Stone for the New World Order. — ***rvb***

The Usual Suspects
Contributors

Melanie Alldrett has been in *Nailed* & *The Gravity of the Thing*, & makes her *GobQ* debut w/ *Follicular Crush/Coqueteo de folicular/Eggbúsbrjóst/Folikularna simpatija* (essay)(ensayo)(ritgerð)(esej) (Eng./Sp./Icel./Croat).

Tânia Cardoso is a Rotterdam-based freelancer whose work incls. comics, ed., *&* scientific *&* children's illustr. She has a Masters in Urbanism fr. Rio's Fed. Uni., & has been a part of street art scenes in Rio, Lisbon, *&* Rotterdam, *&* won the 2014 street art competition *Sesimbra is fish & street art* in Portugal, & the 2017 *Gorsedh Kernow Creativity Award* in Cornwall. Tânia makes her *GobQ* debut w/ *(in)finite/(in)finito* & *loneliness/soledad/solidão* (portfolio).

Ani Gjika, Alb.-Amer. poet *&* tr., is author of *Bread on Running Waters*. Ani returns w/ her Alb. tr. of B. Taulbee's *472 cigarette butts/472 collinas/472 bishta cigaresh/472 opuška/472 окурка*(pome)(poema)(poemë)(pjesma)(тихотворéние) (Eng./Sp./Alb./Croat./Russ.), A. Сен-Сеньков's *Музыка для казни/Glazba za smaknuća/Muzikë për ekzekutime/Music for Executions/Música para las ejecuciones* (стихотворéние)(pjesma)(poemë)(pome)(poema)(Russ./Croat/Alb./Eng./Sp.), M. Kirin's *Gore ne može biti/It Can't Get Much Worse/Не Может Стать Еще Хуже/No puede emporar mucho/Nuk ka më keq* (pjesma)(pome)(стихотворéние)(poema)(poemë (Croat/Eng./Russ./Sp./Alb.),*Drvosječin je posao nevidljiv/The work of a lumberjack is invisible/El trabajo de un leñador es invisible/Puna e një druvari është e padukshme* (pjesma)(pome)(poema)(poemë) (Croat/Eng./Sp./Alb.)

Gintara Grajauskas, whose works incl. 7 pome *&* 2 essay colls., a novel *&* coll. of plays. A select. of pomes, *Then What*, is due fr. Bloodaxe Books (UK) in early 2018. He makes his *GobQ* debut w/*ikonų tapitojas/icon painter/intor de iconos/Slikar ikona*, & *kas yra interneto centre/what there is at the internet's core/lo que hay en el núclea de internet/Što se nalazi u jezgri interneta* (poezija)(pome)(poema)(pjesma) (Lith./Eng./Sp./Croat).

Boris Gregorić returns to *GobQ* w/an Eng. tr. of M. Kirin's *Iz usta mi ispada jezi, i/Mi lengua cae de mi boca/My tongue falls out of my mouth/Mano liežuvis iškrenta man iš burnos* (pjesma)(poema)(pome)(poezija) (Croat/Eng./Sp./Alb.), *Gore ne može biti/It Can't Get Much Worse/He Может Стать Еще Хуже/No puede emporar mucho/Nuk ka më keq* (pjesma)(pome)(стихотворéние)(poema)(poemë)(Croat/Eng./Russ./Sp./Alb.), *Drvosječin je posao nevidljiv/The work of a lumberjack is invisible/El trabajo de un leñador es invisible/Puna e një druvari është e padukshme* (pjesma)(pome)(poema)(poemë)(Croat/Eng./Sp./Alb.), & Eng. tr. of E. Rudan's*u nevremenu/in bad weather/en mal tiempo/bei schlechtem* (pjesma)(pome)(poema)(d.Gedicht) (Croat/Eng./Sp./Germ.), & *Pjesma o junaku nježna srca i vedrih bradavica/The song about the hero with a gentle heart and bright nipples/Canción acerca del héroe con corazón suave y pezones brillantes* (pjesma)(pome)(poema) (Croat/Eng./Sp.).

Dijana Jakovac returns to *GobQ* w/ her Croat tr. of M. Alldritt's *Follicular Crush/Coqueteo de folicular/Eggbúsbrjóst/Folikularna simpatija* (essay)(ensayo)(ritgerð)(esej) (Eng./Sp./Icel./Croat.)

Ana Katana returns to *GobQ* w/ her Croat tr. of *A. Сен-Сеньков Музыка для казни/Glazba za smaknuća/Muzikë për ekzekutime/Music for Executions/Música para las ejecuciones*(стихотворéние)(pjesma)(poemë)(pome)(poema)(Russ./Croat/Alb./Eng./Sp.), B. Taulbee's *472 cigarette butts/472 collinas/472 bishta cigaresh/472 opuška/472 окурка* (pome)(poema)(poemë)(pjesma), *On that couch in the yard, @ the edge of adulthood/Na kauču u dvorištu, na samom rubu odraslosti/En aquel sofá en el patio, al borde de la adultez/На этом диване во дворе, на краю взрослой жизни*, & A. Tellería-Tores' *BCN., Cat., Es.: Cada borde un centro: Oye, tenemos que hablar/BCN, Cat., Sp.: Every Edge a Centre: Hey, We Need to Talk/BCN, Kat., Es.: Serhver Brún Miðju: Við verðdum að tala/BCN., Cat., Es.: Kad je svaki rub središte: Hej, moramo razgovarati* (ensayo)(essay)(ritgerð)(esej) .

Miroslav Kirin returns to *GobQ* w/ *Iz usta mi ispada jezi, i/Mi lengua cae de mi boca/My tongue falls out of my mouth/Mano liežuvis iškrenta man iš burnos* (pjesma)(poema)(pome)(poezija) (crat/Eng./Sp./Alb.), *Gore ne može biti/It Can't Get Much Worse/He Может Стать Еще Хуже/No puede emporar mucho/Nuk ka më keq* (pjesma)(pome)(стихотворéние)(poema)(poemë)(Croat/Eng./Russ./Sp./Alb.), *Drvosječin je posao nevidljiv/The work of a lumberjack is invisible/El trabajo de un leñador es invisible/Puna e një druvari është e padukshme* (pjesma)(pome)(poema)

(poemë) (crat / Eng. / Sp. / Alb.).

Michael Lohr, freq. *GobQ* contrib., returns w/ his Icel. tr. of M. Alldritt's *Follicular Crush/Coqueteo de folicular/ Eggbúsbrjóst/Folikularna simpatija*(essay)(ensayo)(ritgerð) (esej), & A. Tellería-Tores' *Barcelona., Cat., Es.: Cada borde un centro: Oye, tenemos que hablar/BCN, Cat., Sp.: Every Edge a Centre: Hey, We Need to Talk/BCN, Kat., Es.: Serhver Brún Miðju: Við verðdum að tala/BCN., Cat., Es.: Kad je svaki rub središte: Hej, moramo razgovarati* (ensayo)(essay) (ritgerð)(esej)(Sp. / Eng. / Icel. / Croat).(Eng. / Span. / Icel.).

Sergio Morera voted. Did you?

Ainsley Morse & Peter Golub return to *GobQ* w / their Eng. tr. of Андрей Сен-Сеньков's *Музыка для казни/ Glazba za smaknuća/Muzikë për ekzekutime/Music for Executions/Música para las ejecuciones* (стихотворéние)(pjesma) (poemë)(pome)(poema)(Russ. / Croat / Alb. / Eng. / Sp.).

Jelena Pitaki, Croat writer & tr., returns to *GobQ* w / her Croat. tr. of Lith. writer G. Grajauskas' *ikonų tapitojas/icon painter/intor de iconos/Slikar ikona, & kas yra interneto centre/what there is at the internet's core/lo que hay en el núclea de internet, Što se nalazi u jezgri interneta* (poezija)(pome) (poema)(pjesma)

Evelina Rudan's most recent works incl. *Breki i ćuki/Dogs & Owls* (2008)/*Decent Birds* (2008). She makes her *GobQ* w/ *u nevremenu/in bad weather/en mal tiempo/bei schlechtem* (pjesma)(pome)(poema)(d.Gedicht)(Croat / Eng. / Sp. / Germ.), & *Pjesma o junaku nježna srca i vedrih bradavica/The song about the hero with a gentle heart & bright nipples/Canción acerca del héroe con corazón suave y pezones brillantes* (pjesma)(pome)(poema).

Андрей Сен-Сеньков / Andrei Sen-Sekov, living in Moscow, is author of 10+ vols. of pomes & prose, incl. *Anatomical Theater*. He returns w/ *Музыка для казни/ Glazba za smaknuća/Muzikë për ekzekutime/Music for Executions/Música para las ejecuciones* (стихотворéние)(pjesma) (poemë)(pome)(poema)(Russ. / Croat / Alb. / Eng. / Sp.). *Андрей* has also generously done Russ. tr. of B. Taulbee's *How to choose the perfect avocado/Odabrati savršen avokado/ Como escoger el aguacate perfecto /Как выбрать идеальное авокадо*, and *On that couch in the yard, @ the edge of adulthood/Na kauču u dvorištu, na samom rubu odraslosti/En aquel sofá en el patio, al borde de la adultez/На этом диване во дворе, на краю взрослой жизни*(pome)(pjesma)(poema) (тихотворéние)(Eng. / Croat / Sp. / Russ.), *472 cigarette butts/472 collinas/472 bishta cigaresh/472 opuška/472 окурка* (pome)(poema)(poemë)(pjesma)(тихотворéние)(Eng. / Sp. / Croat / Alb. / Russ.), & M. Kirin's *Gore ne može biti/ It Can't Get Much Worse/Не Можем Стать Еще Хуже/ No puede emporar mucho/Nuk ka më keq* (pjesma)(pome) (стихотворéние)(poema)(poemë)(Croat / Eng. / Russ. / Sp. / Alb.)

Džiugas Stanevičius, a student in Vilnius U. Dept. of Tr. Studies BA progr., provides a Lith. tr. of Miroslav Kirin's *Iz usta mi ispada jezi, i/Mi lengua cae de mi boca/My tongue falls out of my mouth/Mano liežuvis iškrenta man iš burnos* (pjesma)(poema) (pome)(poezija) (Croat / Sp. / Eng. / Lith.)

Brenda Taulbee, engaged in post-grad endeavors in San Diego, has been most recently awarded the Sarah B. Marsh-Rebelo Scholarship for Poetry. A freq. *GobQ* contrib., her pome coll., *The Art of Waking Up: 62 Poems & a Song of Despair*, is avail. fr. Reprobate / GobQ Books. She returns to *GobQ* w/ *How to choose the perfect avocado/Odabrati savršen avokado/Como escoger el aguacate perfecto/Как выбрать идеальное авокадо, On that couch in the yard, @ the edge of adulthood/Na kauču u dvorištu, na samom rubu odraslosti/En aquel sofá en el patio, al borde de la adultez/На этом диване во дворе, на краю взрослой жизни*(pome)(pjesma)(poema)(тихотворéние)(Eng. / Croat / Sp. / Russ.), *472 cigarette butts/472 collinas/472 bishta cigaresh/472 opuška/472 окурка* (pome)(poema)(poemë)(pjesma) (тихотворéние) (Eng. / Sp. / Croat / Alb. / Russ.)

Alejandro Tellería-Tores, having lived in Lat. Amer. & Sp., & Londres-based since 2013, is a pub. author (*El rey de la paja*, 2001) who's written for *the Financial Times* & *Al Jazeera Network* since 1995. He makes his *GobQ* debut w/ *BCN., Cat., Es.: Cada borde un centro: Oye, tenemos que hablar/BCN, Cat., Sp.: Every Edge a Centre: Hey, We Need to Talk/BCN, Kat., Es.: Serhver Brún Miðju: Við verðdum að tala/BCN., Cat., Es.: Kad je svaki rub središte: Hej, moramo razgovarati* (ensayo)(essay)(ritgerð)(esej) (Sp. / Eng. / Icel. / Croat).(Eng. / Span. / Icel.).

Rimas Uzgiris, a freq. *GobQ* contrib., teaches lit., tr. & creative writing at Vilnius U. Rimas returns w/ 2 Eng. tr. of Gintara Grajauskas' *ikonų tapitojas/icon painter/pintor de iconos/Slikar ikona, & kas yra interneto centre/what there is at the internet's core/ lo que hay en el núclea de internet, Što se nalazi u jezgri interneta* (poezija)(pome)(poema)(pjesma) (Lith. / Eng. / Sp. / Croat).

Florian Vetsch, a Swiss poet & tr., returns to *GobQ* w/ a Germ. tr. of E. Rudan's *u nevremenu/in bad weather/en mal tiempo/bei schlechtem* (pjesma)(pome)(poema)(d.Gedicht)(Croat / Eng / Sp. / Germ).

Knut Van Brijs, orig. fr. Ghent, but now residing in Sarejevo, makes his *GobQ* debut w/ *Tradition/Traditie/традисуја, & Sufragette/суфрагетме* (bricolage).

T. Warburton y Bajo y rvb did co-tr. of a baker's doz. of this issue's works into Spanish.

Graham Willoughby, whose artwork has adorned our covers since is. 2, returns, & still in watery colour! Graham has exhibited in galleries in the US, Germany & his native Oz, & has artist books in museum colls. worldwide.

Muzikë për ekzekutime

gijotina e parë u prodhua
në ndërmarrjen e klaviçembalëve

midis shumëllojshmëri çelësash
veç ajo është e mprehtë
veç ajo e depërton komplet njeriun
pa prerë si gjithçka tjetër
copat e shëmtuara muzikale derri

— Andrei Sen-Senkov
(Perkthyer ne Shqip nga Anglishtja, Ani Gjika)

Moscow, Russia / Москвá, Россия

МУЗЫКА ДЛЯ КАЗНИ

первую гильотину изготовили
на фабрике клавесинов

среди множества клавишей
только она острая
только она одна проходит человека насквозь
не нарезая как остальные
омерзительные кусочки музыкальной свининки

— Андрей Сен-Сеньков

Glazba za smaknuća

Prva je giljotina proizvedena
U tvornici klavičembala

Među gomilom tipaka
Jedina je ona oštra
Jedina ona sasvim prolazi kroz osobu
Ne režući kao ostale
Užasne komade glazbene svinjetine

— Andrei Sen-Senkov
(prijevod, Jelena Pataki)

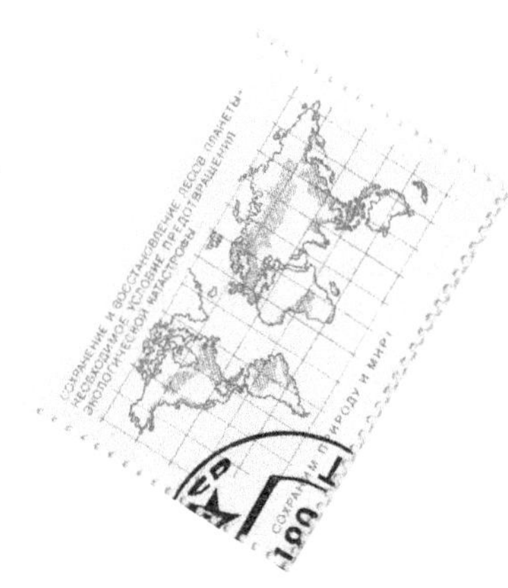

Music for Executions

the first guillotine was produced
at the harpsichord factory

among the multitude of keys
it alone is sharp
it alone passes through a person completely
not cutting like the rest
the hideous pieces of musical pork

— *Andrei Sen-Senkov*
(tr. fr. the Russian, Ainsley Morse & Peter Golub)

Música para las ejecuciones

la primera guillotina fue producido
en la fábrica del clavicordio

entre la multitud de teclas
solo ella es filosa
solo ella pasa a través de una persona totalmente
sin cortar como el resto
las repugnantes piezas de carne de cerdo musical

— *Andrei Sen-Senkov*
(traducción, T. Warburton y Bajo y rub)

Sarajevo / Ghent

Knut Van Brijs,
Suffragette/ суфрагетте, *bricolage* (2017)

Tânia Cardoso,
(in)finite,
comics portfolio

472 cigarette butts

There are 472 cigarette butts
in the side yard adjoining
my neighbor's house and mine.

I know because I left them there.
I have been polluting the air between us
for so long I could practically

call him family.

— Brenda Taulbee

472 colillas

Hay 472 colillas
en el patio de al lado que colinda
la casa de mi vecino y la mía.

lo sé porque yo las dejé allí.
he estado contaminando el aire entre nosotros
durante tanto tiempo que prácticamente podría

llamarlo familia.

— Brenda Taulbee
(traducción, T. Warburton y Bajo y rvb)

472 bishta cigaresh

Janë 472 bishta cigaresh
anash gardhit që lidh
shtëpinë e komshiut tim me timen.

Unë e di pasi unë i lashë ato aty.
E kam mbytur ajrin mes nesh
kaq gjatë saqë praktikisht

e quaj atë familje.

— Brenda Taulbee
(Perkthyer ne Shqip nga Anglishtja, Ani Gjika)

472 opuška

472 opuška leže
U dvorištu koje spaja
Moju kuću sa susjedovom.

Znam jer sam ih ja ostavila tamo.
Zagađujem zrak među nama već tako dugo
Da smo si gotovo

postali obitelj.

— Brenda Taulbee
(Prijevod, Ana Katana)

472 окурка

472 окурка
во дворе, прилегающем
к моему дому и к дому соседа.
Я знаю это, потому что сама оставила их там.
Я загрязняю воздух между нами
так долго, что нас практически можно
назвать одной семьей.

— Бренда Толби
(перевод, Андрей Сен-Сеньков)

Tânia Cardoso,

loneliness / soledad / solidão,

comix portfolio

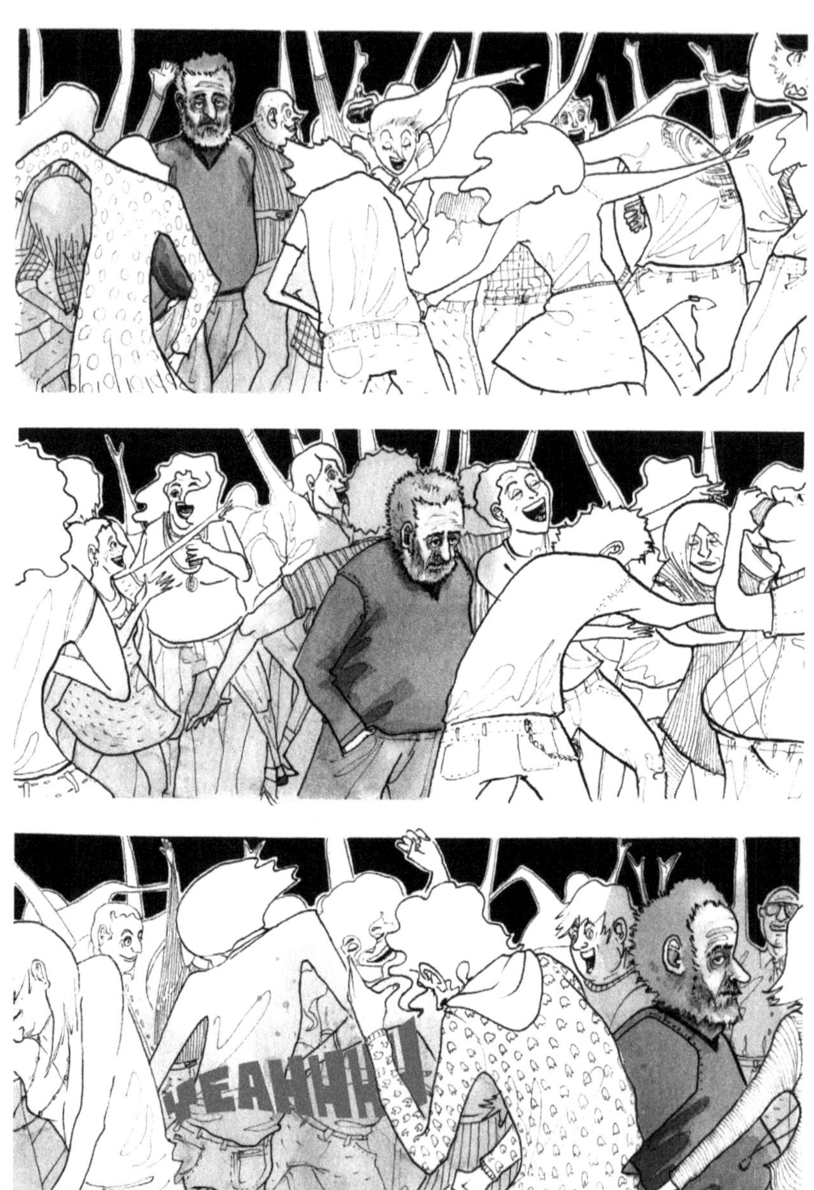
YEAHHH!

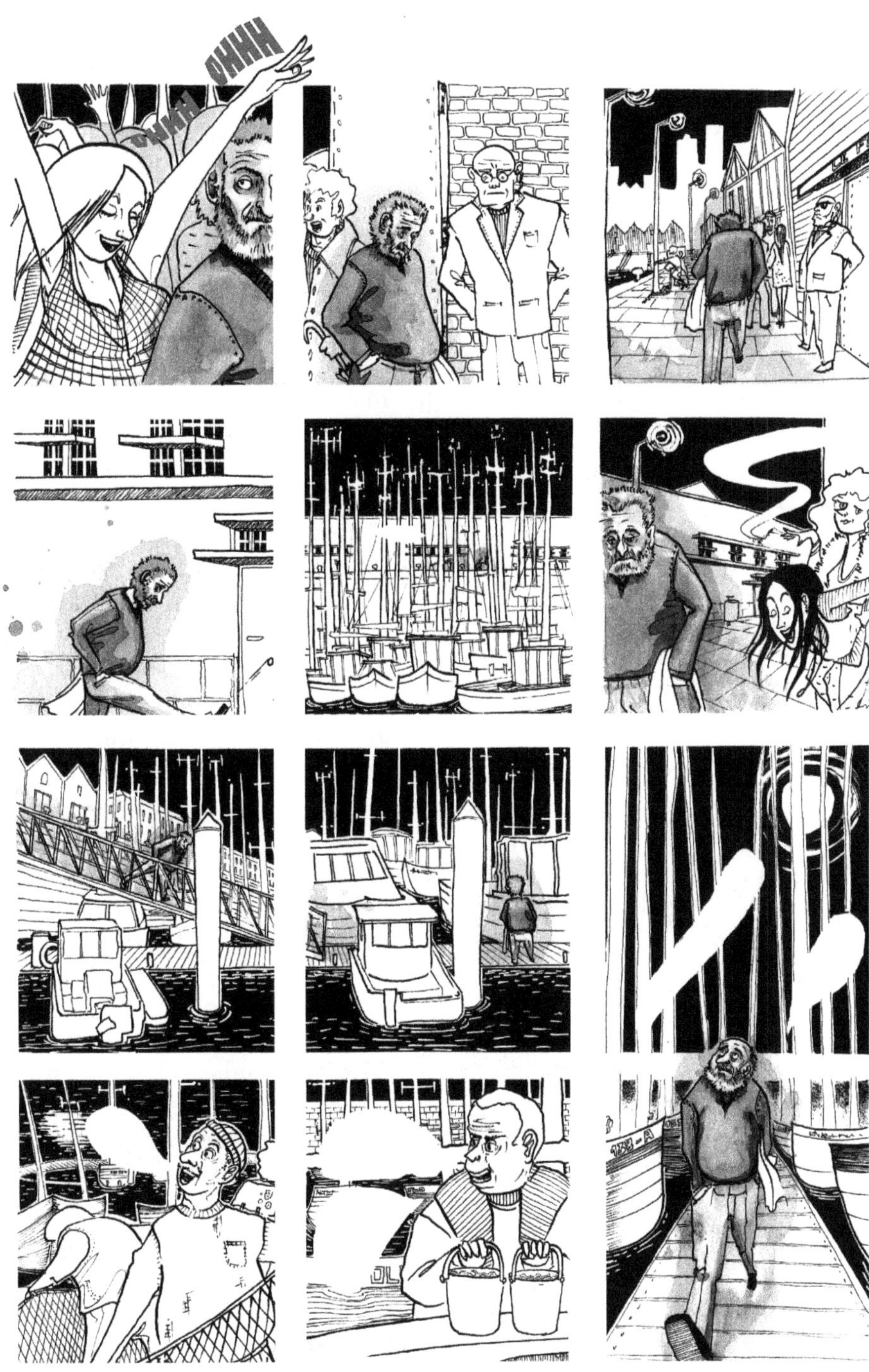
OHHH
OHHH

Follicular Crush

Melanie Alldritt

I'm sitting on the porch at a stranger's house. All I know is that I'm somewhere in town. I'm sitting on a handmade wooden bench that extends from the house across the porch and ends at a wooden railing built a hundred years ago. The hardwood ground of the patio is painted brick red, as is the outside of the house. The railing is a boring tan. My friend is standing next to me smoking a cigarette and talking to me. "Look at her," he says. "Is she your type?"

I tell him I want to touch her hair. But not in the way he thinks. I want to brush my hand against the curls that hide the shoulders of the leopard print costume she's wearing. The costume is the least interesting thing about her. Her outfit could be a pair of footie pajamas, and is completed with a tail that drags on the floor as she walks. I want time to slow down so I can completely observe my right hand reaching from my periphery to touch the thick keratin curls sprouting from her scalp. The potential energy of my hand extended, right above her head in anticipation of resting on the coarse surface will turn into kinetic energy that will transfer to the primary sensory projection area located at the topmost part of her brain and

Coqueteo de folicular

Melanie Alldritt

(traducción, T. Warburton y Bajo y rvb)

Estoy sentada en el porche en casa de un desconocido. Lo único que sé es que estoy en algún lugar de la ciudad. Estoy sentada en un banco de madera hecho a mano que se extiende desde la casa, a través del pórtico y termina en una barandilla de madera construida hace cien años. El piso duro de madera del patio está pintado de color rojo ladrillo, como en el exterior de la casa. El color descolorado del la barandilla es un latté aburrido. Mi amigo está parado junto a mí, fumando un cigarrillo, hablando comigo. "Mira," me dice.¿Ella es tu tipo?"

Le digo que quiero tocar su pelo. Pero no de la manera que piensa. Quiero rozar mi mano contra los rizos que se esconden los hombros del estampado de leopardo traje que lleva. El traje es lo menos interesante de ella. Su vestimenta podría ser un par de calcetines de pijama, completo con una cola que arrastra por el suelo mientras camina. Quiero tiempo para frenar, para poder completanmente observar que mi mano derecha de mi periferia alcanzando a tocar los rizos gruesos brotando de su cuero cabelludo. La energía potencial de mi mano ampliada, directamente encima de su cabeza, en anticipación de descansar en la superficie rugosa se convertirá en energía cinética que se trasladará a las sensoriales primarias área de

Eggbúsbrjóst

Melanie Alldritt
(þýtt úr Ensku, Michael Lohr)

Ég sit á veröndinni í húsi útlendinga. Allt sem ég veit er að ég er einhvers staðar í bænum. Ég sit á handsmíðaðri trébekk sem nær frá húsinu yfir veröndina og endar í trébelg sem byggð var fyrir hundrað árum síðan. The harðviður jörð verönd er máluð múrsteinn rauður, eins og er utan hússins. The rekki er leiðinlegt tan. Vinur minn stendur við hliðina á mér að reykja sígarettu og tala við mig. "Horfðu á hana," segir hann. "Er hún tegund þín?"

Ég segi honum að ég vili snerta hárið. En ekki í því hvernig hann hugsar. Ég vil að bursta höndina mína gegn krulurnar sem fela axlurnar í hlébarði prenta búningnum sem hún er í. Búningurinn er síst áhugaverður hlutur af henni. Útbúnaður hennar gæti verið par af náttfötum, og það er heill með hala sem dregur á gólfið eins og hún gengur. Mig langar til að hægja á mér svo ég geti alveg fylgst með hægri hönd mínum frá útlimum mínum til að snerta þykk keratínkrulla sem spíra frá hársvörð hennar. Hugsanleg orka hönd minnar, sem er rétt fyrir ofan höfuðið í aðdraganda hvíldar á grófu yfirborðinu, mun breytast í hreyfigetu sem mun flytja yfir í aðalskynjunarsvæðinu sem staðsett er efst í heilanum og leyfa henni að skrá sig á annan mann er að snerta hana.

Er hún tegund mín? Það er ekki svo einfalt. Já, það er þessi hugsun. Hún er falleg. Hún minnir mig á einhvern sem ég notaði til dagsetningar. En það snýst

Folikularna simpatija

Melanie Alldritt
(prijevod, Dijana Jakovac)

Sjedim na trijemu u kući stranca. Sve što znam je da sam negdje u gradu. Sjedim na ručno izrađenoj drvenoj klupi koja se proteže od kuće preko puta trijema i završava na drvenoj ogradi napravljenoj prije stotinu godina. Tvrdi drveni pod terase obojen je u nijansi crvene opeke, kao i vanjski dio kuće. Ograda je dosadne žutomrke boje. Prijatelj stoji pored mene, puši cigaretu i razgovara sa mnom. „Pogledaj ju", kaže mi. „Je li ona tvoj tip? "

Kažem mu da želim gladiti njezinu kosu. Ali ne na način na koji on to misli. Želim trljati svoju ruku uz kovrče koje skrivaju ramena haljine leopard uzorka koju nosi. Haljina je najmanje zanimljiva stvar na njoj. Njezina bi odjeća mogla biti i plišana jednodijelna pidžama, upotpunjena repom koji se vuče po podu dok ona hoda. Želim da vrijeme uspori tako da mogu u potpunosti promatrati svoju desnu ruku koja dopire iz periferije moga mozga kako bi dodirnula guste keratinske kovrče koje niču iz njezina vlasišta. Potencijalna energija moje istegnute ruke, točno iznad njezine glave, u očekivanju da će se odmoriti na gruboj površini, pretvorit će se u kinetičku energiju koja će se prenijeti na zonu primarne senzorne projekcije smještene na naj-

allow her to register that another person is touching her.

Is she my type? It's not that simple. Yes, there is that thought. She is beautiful. She reminds me of someone I used to date. But it's not about that. Not really. I want time to nearly freeze and for each second to expand into its own universe. I want to be the photon packages of light reflecting off of her alternately dark brown and reddish curls and passing through my cornea, through my lens and to each retina. I want to feel the rods and cones inside of my eyes process the information of the infinite edges of each strand of hair. As each neuron completes its energy pattern of inputting information to the cellular structures beneath the rods and cones, I will travel with each synapse of information further into my eye, to the back of the retina behind bipolar and ganglion cells to the optic nerve as it leaves each eye.

I want the synchrony of neural function to expand, each parallel universe of energy unfolding spectacularly and precisely before me, small enough to be centered in each fovea so none of the beautifully finite complexity is missed. As groups of cells are stimulated, I desire to feel that which inhibits cellular activity between groups of activation and reveals edges and angles to the cognitive mind. I don't want to ask her out, although if I were drunk I would.

Rather, as the optic nerve travels through to the thalamus to the lateral geniculate nucleus, I long to witness

proyección situada en la parte superior de su cerebro. Le permitirá registrar que otra persona está en contacto con ella.

¿Es mi tipo? No es tan simple. Sí, existe ese piensamiento. Ella es hermosa. Me recuerda a alguien con quien antes salía. Pero no se trata de eso. No realmente. Quiero que el tiempo se congele un poco y que cada segundo se amplié en su propio universo. Quiero ser los paquetes de fotones de luz que reflejan ligero lejos de sus rizos, marrones y rojizas, que pasan a través de mi córnea, a través de mi lente y en cada retina. Quiero sentir los conos y bastones dentro de mis ojos procesar la información de los bordes infinitos de cada hilo del pelo. Como cada neurona termina su patrón de energía de introducción de información en las estructuras celulares por debajo de los bastones y conos, igual, yo viajaré con cadas synapsis de información dentro de mi ojo, en la parte posterior de la retina, detrás de bipolares y las células ganglionares en el nervio óptico, mientras que se escapa de cada ojo.

Quiero que la sincronía de la función neuronal se amplíe, cada universo paralelo de la energía desplegándose espectacularmente y precisamente delante de mí; suficientemente pequeño para centrarse en cada fóvea para que no se pierda la complejidad finita. Como los grupos de células son estimulados, deseo de sentir que lo que inhibe la actividad celular entre los grupos de activación y revela los bordes y ángulos para el mente cognitivo. No quiero invitarla a una noche de aventura, aunque si estuviera bor-

ekki um það. Eiginlega ekki. Ég vil hafa tíma til að frysta næstum og fyrir hverja sekúndu að stækka í eigin alheim. Ég vil vera ljósgjafapakkarnir af ljósi sem endurspegla hana af dökkbrúnum og rauðu krullum og fara í gegnum hornhimnu minn, í gegnum linsuna mína og í hvert sjónhimnu. Mig langar að finna stengurnar og keilurin í augum mínum með því að fá upplýsingar um óendanlega brúnir hvers hárhárra. Þar sem hver tauga lýkur orkusmynni þess að setja inn upplýsingar í frumuuppbygginguna undir stöngunum og keilurunum, mun ég ferðast með hverri synjun upplýsinga frekar í augað mitt, að baki sjónhimnanna á bak við geðhvarfasýki og gangljónfrumur í sjóntaugakerfið eins og það skilur hvert augað.

Ég vil samstillingu taugaþáttarins að stækka, hvert samhliða alheimur orku þróast stórfenglega og einmitt fyrir mig; nógu lítið til að vera miðstöðvar í hverri fovea svo að enginn af fallega endanlegu flóknu sé saknað. Eins og frumufjöldur örva, langar mig til að finna það sem hamlar frumuvirkni milli virkjunarhópa og sýnir brúnir og horn til vitrænnar huga. Ég vil ekki spyrja hana, þó að ég væri drukkinn. Frekar, þar sem sjóntaugakerfið ferðast í gegnum thalamus til hliðar mótefna kjarnans, langar mig til að verða vitni að getu heila til að greina og mótmæla mótmæla sem eiga sér stað í miðju forræðisins, undir cortical vefjum sem springur með trilljónfrumum. Ég mun ferðast með sérhverjum taugaþrýstingi frá dendríti í gegnum frumu líkamann til axonsins þar sem það verður taugaboðefnið af synaptic hleypa og endurtakar ferlið og stuðlar að boðinu áfram. Jafnvel synapses sem miðla footie

gornjem dijelu mozga i omogućiti joj da osvijesti da ju druga osoba dodiruje.

Je li ona moj tip? Nije to tako jednostavno. Da, postoji takva misao. Ona je prekrasna. Podsjeća me na nekoga s kime sam bila hodala. Ali ne radi se o tome. Ne baš. Želim da se vrijeme gotovo zamrzne i da se svaka sekunda proširi u svoj vlastiti svemir. Želim biti fotonski paket svjetlosti koji se odbija od njezinih naizmjenično tamnosmeđih i crvenkastih kovrča i koji prolazi kroz rožnicu moga oka, kroz moje leće pa sve do mrežnice. Želim osjetiti štapiće i čunjiće unutar svojih očiju kako obrađuju informacije o beskonačnim rubovima svakog pramena kose. Kao što svaki neuron dovršava svoj energetski uzorak uvođenja informacija na stanične strukture ispod štapića i čunjića, ja ću sa svakom sinapsom informacija putovati sve dalje u svoje oko, na stražnju stranu mrežnice iza bipolarnih i ganglijskih stanica do optičkog živca.

Želim da se sinkronizacija neuronske funkcije proširi, da se svaki paralelni svemir energije rasprostre spektakularno i točno ispred mene; dovoljno malen da bude u središtu svake fovee tako da nijedna prekrasno ograničena složenost ne bude propuštena. Kao što se skupine stanica stimuliraju, čeznem da osjetim što je to što koči staničnu aktivnost između grupa aktivacije i otkriva rubove i uglove do kognitivnog uma. Ne želim je pozvati na spoj, iako, da sam pijana, pozvala bih je.

the brain's capabilities of object recognition and interpretation that occur in the center of the forebrain, beneath the cortical tissue that is bursting with a trillion cells. I will travel with each nerve synapse from dendrite through the cell body to the axon where it becomes a neurotransmitter from synaptic firing and repeats the process, furthering the message onward. Even the synapses that communicate the footie pajamas.

Finally, as the optic nerve continues to travel back to the occipital cortex to V1 where the information of sight is further broken down and sent across the cortex to the temporal, parietal and frontal lobes, I want to split myself into infinite pieces to engage in parallel processing in each area of brain that is bursting with energy and oxygen from blood flow. This should be felt without the sense of urgency that comes with the reality that these synchronic processes occur all at the same time and within a second. Recognition of sight is complete in such a gorgeously small fraction of time, but not here. In the second that it takes for her to lift her arm to her face to take a drag of her cigarette, her hair separates into two blankets: one on her back, the other on her chest. I will dually witness the movement of hair and follow each step of neural processing in my mind, because time will nearly freeze and I will be left to ecstatically experience each reality individually and as part of the whole.

It's not that I just want to touch her racha si lo quisiera.

Más bien, cuando el nervio óptico viaja a través del tálamo hasta el núcleo geniculado lateral, añoro ser testigo de las capacidades del cerebro de reconocimiento, de objetos y de la interpretación que se producen en el centro del prosencéfalo, debajo del tejido cortical que se revienta con un trillón de las células. Viajaré con cada sinapsis del nervio de dendrita a través del cuerpo de la célula al axón donde se convierte en un neurotransmisor de disparas sinápticas y repite el proceso, fomentando el mensaje hacia afuera. Incluso las sinapsis que comunican las pijamitas.

Finalmente, como el nervio óptico sigue viajando detrás de la corteza occipital-V1, donde la información de la vista es dividida adelante y enviada a través de la corteza a los lóbulos temporal y parietal y frontales, quiero yo dividirme en partes infinitas para participar en el procesamiento paralelo en cada área del cerebro que se revienta con energía y oxígeno del flujo sanguíneo. Esto se debe sentirse sin el mismo sentido de la urgencia que viene con la realidad de que estos procesos sincrónicos ocurren todos al mismo tiempo, y dentro de un segundo. El reconocimiento de la visión se complete en una preciosa pequeña fracción de tiempo, pero no aquí. En el segundo que se toma levantar el brazo a su cara para tomar una rastra de su cigarrillo, su pelo se separa en dos mantas; uno en su espalda y el otro en su pecho. Doblemente, presentiré el movimiento de pelo y seguiré cada paso del procesamiento neural en mi mente, porque el tiempo

náttfötunum.

Að lokum, þar sem sjóntaugakerfið heldur áfram að fara aftur í hjartakvilla til V1, þar sem upplýsingarnar um sjón eru frekar sundurliðaðar og sendar yfir heilaberki til tímabundna, parietal og frontal lobes, vil ég skipta mér í óendanlega hluti til að taka þátt í samhliða vinnsla á hverju svæði heilans sem springur af orku og súrefni frá blóðflæði. Þetta ætti að líða án þess að brýna nauðsyn beri að veruleika að þessi samstilltu ferli eiga sér stað allt á sama tíma og innan seinna. Viðurkenning sjónar er lokið í svona gorgeously lítill brot af tíma, en ekki hér. Í öðru lagi sem það tekur að henni að lyfta handleggnum í andlit hennar til að draga á sígarettu sínu skilur hárið í tvö teppi; einn á bakinu, hitt á brjósti hennar. Ég mun tvíhliða verða vitni um hárið á hreyfingu og fylgja hverju þrepi tauga vinnslu í huga mínum, því að tíminn mun nánast frjósa og ég mun vera vinstri til að meta hverrar veruleika einstaklega og sem hluta af heildinni.

Það er ekki það sem ég vil bara snerta hárið. Eða að ég vili verða vitni til varamanna, undirmeðvitaðra veruleika sem hugurinn minn tekur þátt í hverri sekúndu og aðeins leyfir mér að sjá fullunna vöru. Það er ekki einu sinni sem vinur minn vill sjá mig fara heim með hana svo að hann geti gefið mér vitleysa um það næsta dag.

Það er bara það sem ég vil taka þátt í. Alveg þátt. Ég vil vera svo til staðar á hverju óendanlegu plani sem á sér stað samtímis að húðin mín snýr heitt með styrkleika þekkingar og orku og hugurinn minn getur haldið innri og ytri heimi í einu fallegu augnablikinu. Mig langar að veruleika að stækka

Umjesto toga, kao što optički živac putuje kroz talamus do jezgre lateralnog genikuluma, žudim da svjedočim sposobnostima mozga u prepoznavanju i tumačenju objekata koji se javljaju u središnjem dijelu prednjega mozga, ispod kortikalna koštana tkiva koje se rasipa s trilijun stanica. Putovat ću sa svakom sinapsom živaca od dendrita kroz stanično tijelo do aksona kada nastaje neurotransmiter od pucanja sinapsi te se ponavlja postupak, unapređujući dalje poruke. Čak i sa sinapsama koje obavještavaju plišane jednodijelne pidžame.

Konačno, kao što optički živac nastavlja putovati natrag do vidne kore mozga, do vidnog područja 1, gdje se podaci o vidu dalje razgrađuju i šalju preko kore mozga do temporalnog, parijetalnog i frontalnog režnja, želim se rascjepkati u beskonačne dijelove kako bih se uključila u paralelno procesiranje u svakom području koje se rasipa energijom i kisikom iz protoka krvi. To bi se trebalo osjetiti bez osjećaja hitnosti koja dolazi s realnošću da se ovi sinkronijski procesi pojavljuju u isto vrijeme u sekundi. Vidno je prepoznavanje dovršeno u tako sjajno malenom djeliću vremena, ali ne ovdje. U djeliću sekunde koji joj je potreban da podigne ruku na lice kako bi povukla dim cigarete, njezina se kosa dijeli na dva prekrivača; jednoga na leđima, drugoga na prsima. Ja ću dvojno svjedočiti kretanju kose i slijediti svaki korak neuronskog procesiranja u svojem umu, jer će se vrijeme gotovo zamrznuti i ja ću biti prepuštena da

hair. Or that I want to witness the alternate, subconscious reality that my mind engages in each second and only allows me sight of the finished product. It's not even that my friend wants to see me go home with her so he can give me crap about it the next day.

It's just that I want to be involved. Fully involved. I want to be so present on each infinite plane that occurs simultaneously that my skin turns hot with the intensity of knowledge and energy and my mind can hold the internal and external worlds in one beautiful moment. I want reality to expand outward with infinite complexity and for my body to be dually large with the internal and small with recognition of the size of the physical globe. When this woman with fantastic hair recognizes both physically and neurologically that I am touching her and her energy shifts as she turns to greet me, I want the physical connection to evolve into verbal. Maybe. Maybe not.

As I contemplate whether or not I should approach her because, as my friend says, "She's totally gay and your type," that question of interaction shrinks in the potential that lies where science departs from concrete reality and into quantum physics. This is the glorious point where nothing is truly known and everything becomes possible because what is "known" is reduced to patterns with both varying predictability and testability. It is here, right here, that I want to be.

casi se congela y me quedare con esta experiencia extasiada de cada realidad individual y a la vez parte de un todo.

No es solamente que quiero tocar su pelo. O que quiero dar testimonio de la realidad alternativa y subconsciente que mi mente se dedica en cada segundo y solo me permite ver el producto acabado. Ni siquiera es que mi amigo quiere ver que me la llevo a mi casa, solo por bromearme sin piedad sobre ella al día siguiente.

Solamente es que quiero estar implicado. Totalmente implicado. Yo quiero ser tan presente en cada plano infinito que se produce al mismo tiempo que mi piel se vuelve caliente con la intensidad de los conocimientos y la energía y la mente pueden sostener los mundos internos y externos en un momento hermoso. Quiero que la realidad se amplié hacia el exterior con la infinita complejidad y que mi cuerpo sea dualmente grande con los internos y los pequeños, con el reconocimiento del tamaño del mundo físico. Cuando esta mujer con el pelo fantástico reconoce físicamente y neurológicamente que la estoy tocando y su energía se traslada a saludarme, yo quiero que la conexión física se convertía a verbal. Tal vez. Tal vez no.

Al contemplar si debo o no debo acercarme a ella porque, como dice mi amigo, "ella es totalmente gay, y de tu tipo", esa pregunta de la interacción se encoge en el potencial que se encuentra donde la ciencia se aparta de la realidad concreta y en la física cuántica. Este es el punto glorioso en que nada es realmente conocido y

út með óendanlegu flókið og að líkaminn minn sé stórlega stór með innri og smári með viðurkenningu á stærð jarðarinnar. Þegar þessi kona með frábært hár viðurkennir bæði líkamlega og taugafræðilega að ég snerti hana og orku vaktir hennar þegar hún snýr að því að heilsa mér, vil ég líkamlega tengingu þróast í munnleg. Gæti verið. Kannski ekki.

Eins og ég hugleiði hvort ég ætti að nálgast hana vegna þess að eins og vinur minn segir: "Hún er algerlega gay og tegundin þín," þá spyr þessi spurning um samskipti hugsanlegan möguleika sem liggur þar sem vísindi fara frá steypu veruleika og í skammtafræði. Þetta er glæsilega staðurinn þar sem ekkert er sannarlega vitað og allt verður mögulegt vegna þess að það sem er "þekkt" er minnkað í mynstur með bæði mismunandi fyrirsjáanleika og prófunarhæfni. Það er hér, hérna, sem ég vil vera.

Það er hér að verkum sjónrænrar viðurkenningar og skilnings verða minna áþreifanleg og fulltrúi möguleika þess að lífið líkist vísindum og vísindum líkist lífið. Ef maður lítur nógu vel út, er það á þessum tímapunkti að möguleiki hvers sjálfstæðs veruleika undanskilist ástæðu og rökfræði og hugsun. Það er á þessum tímapunkti að ég geti setið í ótta við fegurðina sem ég veit ekki en ég er forréttinda að skoða, jafnvel þótt það sé bara í eina sekúndu.

Þegar ég situr á þessari handgerðu trébekk með rauðum stilettunum mínum á gólfinu undir hnjám mínum og sígarettu í hendi minni við hliðina á vini mínum sem vill sjá mig gera hreyfingu á útlendingi, hlé ég. Ekki að ekstatički proživljavam svaku stvarnost i pojedinačno i kao dio cjeline.

Nije da samo želim gladiti njezinu kosu. Ili da želim svjedočiti alternativnoj, podsvjesnoj stvarnosti kojom se moj um bavi svake sekunde i dopušta mi samo viđenje gotovog proizvoda. Nije čak ni da me moj prijatelj želi vidjeti kako odlazim doma s njom da bi mi sutradan mogao spočitavati.

Samo želim biti uključena. Potpuno uključena. Želim biti prisutna na svakoj beskrajnoj ravnini koja se istodobno javlja da moja koža može uzavrjeti intenzitetom znanja i energije, a da moj um može držati unutarnje i vanjske svjetove u jednom predivnom trenutku. Želim da se stvarnost širi prema van s beskonačnom složenošću i da moje tijelo bude dvostruko veliko s unutrašnjošću i malo s priznanjem veličine fizičkog globusa. Kada ova žena bajne kose uoči i fizički i neurološki da je dodirujem i da se njezina energija mijenja kada se okrene da me pozdravi, želim da se tjelesna povezanost razvije u verbalnu. Možda. Možda i ne.

Dok razmišljam hoću li joj prići ili ne, jer, kako kaže moj prijatelj:

„Ona je totalno gej i tvoj je tip," to pitanje interakcije skuplja se u mogućnosti koja leži gdje znanost odstupa od konkretne stvarnosti u kvantnoj fizici. Ovo je veličanstveni trenutak kada ništa nije uistinu poznato i kada sve postaje moguće jer ono što je „poznato" svodi se na uzorke s varirajućom predvidljivosti i ispitljivosti. Ovdje je, upravo ovdje, gdje želim biti.

It is here that the workings of visual recognition and cognition become less concrete and representative of the possibility that life resembles science and science resembles life. If one looks hard enough, it is at this point that the potential of each independent reality subsumes reason and logic and thought. It is at this point that I can sit in awe of the beauty of that which I don't know but am privileged to view, even if it is just for a single second.

As I sit on this handmade wooden bench with my red stilettos on the floor beneath my knees and a cigarette in my hand next to my friend that wants to see me make a move on a stranger, I pause. Not to contemplate my potential move, not to think of what to say, not to notice her body or to picture her naked or what it would look like if I pulled her hair until her lips were in front of mine to kiss. None of these things. I pause because I want to feel the rushing of what it is to be fully present on every level of cellular and physical recognition. Because in these neurological and physical processes, if one looks hard enough, the desire to be infinite and omniscient can be a reality. Just for the smallest fraction of a second. *Q*

todo se vuelve posible porque lo que "se conocido" es reducido a modelos tanto con diferentes previsibilidad y verificabilidad. Es aquí, justo aquí, adonde quiero estar.

Es aquí el lugar en el que el funcionamiento de reconocimiento visual y la cognición se vuelven menos concretas y representante de la posibilidad de que la vida se parece a la ciencia y la ciencia se parece a la vida. Si uno parece bastante difícil, está a este punto que el potencial de cada realidad independiente subsume la razón y la lógica y el pensamiento. En ese punto, me puedo sentar en el temor de la belleza de la que no lo sé pero soy privilegiada de ver, aunque sólo dure por un solo segundo.

Mientras que estoy sentado en este banco de madera hecho a mano con mis tacones rojos en el piso debajo de mis rodillas, y un cigarrillo en mi mano, junto a mi amigo que quiere verme hacer una movida a una desconocida, me detengo. No es para contemplar mi movimiento potencial, ni para pensar en qué decir, ni fijarme en su cuerpo o imaginarla desnuda, ni para ver qué pasaría si le jalo su pelo para besarsla. Ninguna de estas cosas. Hago una pausa porque quiero sentir el torrente de lo que es estar totalmente presente en cada nivel del reconocimiento celular y físico. Como en estos procesos físicos y neurológicos, si uno busca lo suficiente, el deseo de ser infinito y omnisciente puede ser una realidad. Sólo para la más pequeña fracción de un segundo. *Q*

hugleiða hugsanlega hreyfingu mína, ekki að hugsa um hvað ég á að segja, ekki að taka eftir líkama hennar eða að mynda hana nakinn eða hvað það myndi líta út ef ég dró hárið á hana þar til varir hennar voru fyrir framan mín til að kyssa. Ekkert af þessum hlutum. Ég hlé vegna þess að ég vil að þjóta af því að það sé að vera fullkomlega til staðar á öllum stigum frumu og líkamlegrar viðurkenningar. Vegna þess að í þessum taugafræðilegum og líkamlegum ferlum, ef maður lítur nógu vel út, þá er löngunin að vera óendanlegur og alvitur að veruleika. Bara fyrir minnstu brot af sekúndu.

Þegar ég situr á þessari handgerðu trébekk með rauðum stilettunum mínum á gólfinu undir hnjám mínum og sígarettu í hendi minni við hliðina á vini mínum sem vill sjá mig gera hreyfingu á útlendingi, hlé ég. Ekki að hugleiða hugsanlega hreyfingu mína, ekki að hugsa um hvað ég á að segja, ekki að taka eftir líkama hennar eða að mynda hana nakinn eða hvað það myndi líta út ef ég dró hárið á hana þar til varir hennar voru fyrir framan mín til að kyssa. Ekkert af þessum hlutum. Ég hlé vegna þess að ég vil að þjóta af því að það sé að vera fullkomlega til staðar á öllum stigum frumu og líkamlegrar viðurkenningar. Vegna þess að í þessum taugafræðilegum og líkamlegum ferlum, ef maður lítur nógu vel út, þá er löngunin að vera óendanlegur og alvitur að veruleika. Bara fyrir minnstu brot af sekúndu. Q

Ovdje djelovanja vizualnog prepoznavanja i spoznavanja postaju manje konkretna i reprezentativna o mogućnosti da život nalikuje znanosti i da znanost nalikuje životu. Ako pogledate bolje, u ovom trenutku mogućnost svake neovisne stvarnosti uključuje razum, logiku i misao. U ovom trenutku mogu sjediti diveći se ljepoti koju ne poznajem, ali je imam privilegiju gledati, pa makar to trajalo samo sekundu.

Dok sjedim na ovoj ručno izrađenoj drvenoj klupi sa svojim crvenim štiklama na podu i pored koljena te s cigaretom u ruci pokraj prijatelja koji želi da napravim prvi korak sa strancem, zastajem. Ne da razmišljam o svom mogućem potezu, ne da mislim što ću reći, ne da primjećujem njezino tijelo ili da je zamišljam golu ili kako bi to izgledalo kada bih povukla njezinu kosu sve dok njezine usne ne bi bile ispred mojih da ih poljubim. Nijedna od tih stvari. Zastajem jer želim osjetiti bujicu toga kako je to biti u potpunosti prisutan na svakoj razini staničnog i fizičkog prepoznavanja. Zato što u ovim neurološkim i fizičkim procesima, ako bolje pogledate, želja da budete beskonačni i sveznajući može biti stvarnost. Samo u najmanjem djeliću sekunde. Q

НЕ МОЖЕТ СТАТЬ ЕЩЕ ХУЖЕ

Наверху дребезжат окна
По кухне раскатились яблоки
Телевизор выключился сам по себе
Масло разлилось по полу
На висящей на стене картинке исчезло дерево
Я думаю понимаю что происходит
Но прячусь за çерево
Не зная откуда позвонить

— Мирослав Кирин
(перевóд, Андрей Сен-Сеньков)

Zagreb, Hrvatska / Croatia

Gore ne može biti

Gore prozori kloparaju
U kuhinji su se pomakle jabuke
Televizor se sam ugasio
Ulje se prolilo po podu
Na slici na zidu nestalo je stablo
Mislim da znam što se događa
Ali sakrio sam se iza stabla
Ne znam odakle da vam se javim

— Miroslav Kirin

It Can't Get Much Worse

Upstairs the windows rattle
In the kitchen the apples moved
The TV turned itself off
Oil spilled across the floor
On the wall's picture a tree has disappeared
I think I know what's going on
But I hide behind the tree
Not knowing from whence to call

— Miroslav Kirin
(tr. fr. the Croatian, Boris Gregorić)

No puede emporar mucho

arriba las ventanas traquetean
en la cocina las manzanas se movieron
el televisión se apagadó automáticamente
aceite se derramó por el piso
en la foto en la pared un árbol ha desaparecido
creo que sé lo que está pasando
pero me escondo detrás del árbol
sin saber de dónde llamar

— *Miroslav Kirin*
(traducción, T. Warburton y Bajo y rvb)

Nuk ka më keq

Në katin sipër rrapëllijnë dritaret
Në kuzhinë mollët lëvizën
Televizori shuajti veten
Vaj u derdh përgjatë dyshemese
Brënda pikturës në mur është zhdukur një pemë
Më duket se e di ç'po ndodh
Por fshihem pas pemës
Duke mos ditur se nga të thërras.

— *Miroslav Kirin*
(Perkthyer ne Shqip nga Anglishtja, Ani Gjika)

Iz usta mi ispada jezik

iz usta mi ispada jezik
to više nije jezik to je golema jetra teleća onog teleta što su ga zaklali prekjučer
uvjerava me mesar moje omiljene mesnice ali ja u mesnicu niti nisam otišao
nemam ni omiljenu mesnicu
samo mi je jezik ispao iz usta ta golema jetra
vraćam je u usta guram u grlo
odustajem kad shvatim da me guši
moj jezik ponovno ispada
vješa se plazi po vratu liže tijelo
moj jezik moj jezik moj preveliki jezik

— *Miroslav Kirin*

My tongue falls out of my mouth

My tongue falls out of my mouth
It is no longer a tongue, it is a huge calf's liver
of the calf we slaughtered yesterday
the butcher of my favorite butcher shop assures me
But I didn't go to the butcher shop
and neither do I have a favorite butcher shop
It is my tongue that has fallen out of my mouth
This huge liver
I'm putting it back pushing it into my throat
I give up when I realize that it is choking me
My tongue falls out again
hangs onto me creeps up my neck licks my body
Through my tongue through my tongue through my most grievous tongue

— *Miroslav Kirin*
(Tr. fr. the Croatian, Boris Gregorić & M. Kirin)

Mi lengua cae de mi boca

Mi lengua cae de mi boca
es no más una lengua es un enorme hígado del
ternero que hemos sacrificado el día de ayer
el carnicero de mi carnicería favorita me asegura
pero no fui a la carnicería
y tampoco tengo una carnicero favorita
es mi lengua que ha caído de mi boca
este hígado enorme
lo estoy regresando de nuevo empujándolo en mi garganta
me doy por vencido cuando me doy cuenta de que me está ahogando
mi lengua cae otra vez
y cuelga sobre mí, sube sigilosamente por mi cuello, lame mi cuerpo
por mi lengua por mi lengua por mi más dolorosa lengua

— *Miroslav Kirin*
(traducción, T. Warburton y Bajo y rvb)

Mano liežuvis iškrenta man iš burnos

Mano liežuvis iškrenta man iš burnos,
tačiau tai jau nebe liežuvis, o didžiulio veršiuko kepenys,
veršiuko, kurį mes vakar papjovėm,
patikino mane mano mėgstamiausios mėsinės mėsininkas.
Tačiau nėjau į jokią mėsinę,
ir apskritai neturiu mėgstamiausios mėsinės.
Tai mano liežuvis, šios didžiulės kepenys,
iškrito man iš burnos,
dedu į burną ir stumiu atgal į gerklę,
pasiduodu, kai suprantu, kad jis mane dusina.
Mano liežuvis vėl iškrenta,
prikimba prie manęs, šliaužia kaklu ir laižo mano kūną.
Per liežuvį, per mano liežuvį, per mano varganą liežuvį.

— Miroslav Kirin
(Vertė Džiugas Stanevičius)

Drvosječin je posao nevidljiv

U ponoć netko siječe drva.
Preko rijeke stiže tek mjesečeva svjetlost.
Razmišljamo sve do jutra.
A onda – stop. Nema dalje.

— *Miroslav Kirin*

The work of a lumberjack is Invisible

At midnight someone is chopping wood.
From across the river the reaching moonshine.
We think and think until the morning hour.
And then — we stop. Nothing else.

— *Miroslav Kirin*
(tr. fr. the Croatian, Boris Gregorić)

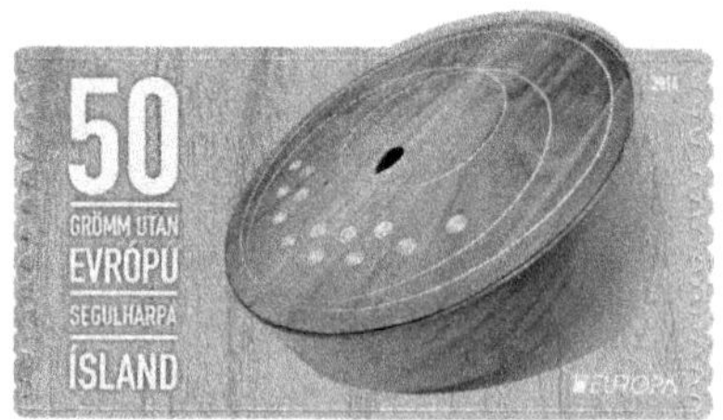

El trabajo de un leñador es invisible

A la medianoche alguien corta leña.
Desde el otro lado del río el alcance de la luna.
pensamos y pensamos hasta la hora de mañana.
y luego – nos detenemos. Nada más.

— *Miroslav Kirin*
(traducción, T. Warburton y Bajo y rvb)

Puna e një druvari është e padukshme

Në mesnatë dikush pre dru.
Që përtej lumit dritë e hënës mbrrin.
Ne mendojmë e mendojmë thellë deri në agim.
Dhe pastaj – pushojmë. Kurrfarë gjë më shumë.

— *Miroslav Kirin*
(Perkthyer ne Shqip nga Anglishtja, Ani Gjika)

Barcelona, Catalonia, España: Cada borde un centro: Oye, tenemos que hablar

Alejandro Tellería-Tores

Perdonadme el egoísmo: me preocupan las cosas en mi casa. Ayer mis hijos volvieron a discutir por no se qué mierda de niños, que discuten cada día por cosas de niños de mierda. La pelea era algo así como que uno le decía al otro: 'Tú sí', y el otro contestaba: 'Yo no'. Llegaron a las manos y con las manos se llegaron a las caras.

El presentador de televisión Berto Romero empezaba el programa Late Motiv del martes 3 de octubre –un show de la conversación nocturno de alta audiencia– de esta manera, equiparando en su monólogo inicial la tensión entre Cataluña y España con una pelea de niños. En el referendo independentista del domingo anterior, calificado por el gobierno central como ilegal y conocido en el país como 1-O, la actuación del gobierno del Partido Popular para manejar el desafío nacionalista fue deplorable: las fuerzas policiales combinadas enviadas desde Madrid se emplearon

Barcelona, Catalonia, Spain: Every Edge A Centre: Hey, We Need to Talk

Alejandro Tellería-Tores
(tr. fr. the Spanish, A. Tellería-Tores)

"Forgive my selfishness: I worry about things in my house. Yesterday my children started arguing once again about I do not know what sort of kids' shit, who argue every day about childish shit. The quarrel was something like one telling the other, 'you do', and the other replying, 'I don't.' The fisticuff started from hand to hand, but soon evolved to their faces."

Last October 3rd TV presenter Berto Romero opened *Late Motiv* — a high-audience late night talkshow — with this monologue, equating the tension between Catalonia and Spain with a kiddie fight. In the *independentista* referendum of the previous Sunday, deemed illegal by the central government and known all over the country as 1-O, the Popular Party (PP)'s/government's handling of the separatist challenge was deplorable: the combined police forces sent from Madrid responded harshly to population that only claimed their right to

Barcelona, Katalónía, España: Sérhver Brún Miðju: Við verðum að tala

Alejandro Tellería-Tores
(þýtt úr Ensku, Michael Lohr)

"Fyrirgefðu eigingirni mína: Ég hef áhyggjur af hlutum í húsi mínu. Í gær byrjaði börnin mín að rifja upp aftur um að ég veit ekki hvers konar skít barna, sem halda því fram daglega um barnalegan skít. Ágreiningurinn var eins og sá að segja öðrum, "*þú gerir*" og hinn svarar: "*Ég geri það ekki.*" Fisticuff byrjaði frá hendi til hönd, en fljótlega þróast í andlit þeirra."

Berto Romero kynnti síðasta þriðjudagskvöld 3 Tveir Motiv — hátíðarmaður seint kvöld talk-show — með þessari einróma sem jafngildir spennu milli Katalóníu og Spánar með kiddie berjast. Í independentista þjóðaratkvæðagreiðslu síðasta sunnudags, sem talið var ólöglegt af stjórnvöldum og þekkt um allt landið sem 1-0, var aðgerð stjórnvalda hins opinbera að takast á við aðskilnaðarspurningin hrikaleg: Sameinuðu lögreglustöðvar sendar frá Madrid reyndi hart að svara íbúum sem höfðu aðeins krafist réttar þeirra til að ákveða, yfirgefa meira en 800 særðir og koma í

Barcelona, Catalonia, España: Kad je svaki rub središte: Hej, moramo razgovarati

Alejandro Tellería-Tores
(pr. s engleskoga, Ana Katana)

"Ispričavam se zbog svoje sebičnosti: brinu me moji ukućani. Jučer su se moja djeca ponovno posvađala zbog kojekavih dječjih sranja, a svaki dan se svađaju zbog istih takvih djetinjastih sranja. Svađali su se onako kao kad jedan govori 'jesi', a drugi odgovara, 'nisam.' Isprva je šaka tukla šaku, no ubrzo su prešli na lica."

TV voditelj Berto Romero je 3. listopada otvorio *Late Motiv* — popularni kasnovečernji *talk show* — upravo ovim monologom, izjednačavajući tako španjolsko-katalonska neslaganja sa dječjom svađom. U *independentista* referendumu protekle nedjelje, kojeg je centralna vlada proglasila ilegalnim i koji je diljem zemlje poznat kao 1-0, postupak vlade Narodne stranke (PP) za rješavanje separatističkog pitanja bio je gađenja vrijedan: kombinirane policijske snage poslane iz Madrida su grubo odgovorile narodu koji je tražio

con dureza contra una población que solo reclamaba su derecho a decidir, y dejaron más de ochocientos heridos, impidiendo el voto de 750.000 personas por la incautación policial de urnas electorales según cifras de la Generalitat de Catalunya.

Por supuesto que el gobierno catalán debió haber organizado un referendo legal y no la burrada trágica del domingo, que ha implicado serios riesgos de seguridad desde el principio y que incluso ya había sido valorado como "catástrofe" por las alcaldesas de Madrid y Barcelona, Manuela Carmena y Ada Colau, en una entrevista hace menos de dos semanas. La Generalitat se saltó a la torera la Constitución política que debatió, aceptó, aprobó y firmó con España luego del final de la dictadura de Francisco Franco, con la intención de reavivar sueños pospuestos de independencia en la población catalana, que ha crecido con políticas educativas autonómicas que aun a día de hoy incentivan en ella sentimientos locales muy virulentos contra el Estado, el idioma y todo lo español.

Mientras tanto, la España contemporánea no tiene empacho en mostrarse como un país de modelos desfasados y hasta arcaicos de democracia y políticas públicas, que abren sus puertas a innumerables casos de corrupción de funcionarios y malversación de fondos en la mayoría de comunidades autónomas, incluida Cataluña, que también ha suf-

decide. According to figures from the autonomous government central body Generalitat in Barcelona, the police seizure of ballot boxes left more than 800 injured and prevented the vote of 750,000 people.

Of course the Catalan government should have organized a legal referendum and not the tragic mêlée run last 1-O, which entailed serious security risks from the outset and had even been previously evaluated in a TV interview a few weeks ago as a "catastrophe" by both Madrid and Barcelona mayors, Manuela Carmena and Ada Colau. The Generalitat deliberately pole-vaulted the political Constitution they had debated, accepted, approved and signed with Spain in 1978 after the end of Gen Francisco Franco's military dictatorship, with the intention of reviving postponed dreams of independence in a Catalan electorate which had been raised with self-ruled educational policies. To this day, these policies encourage virulent local feelings against the state, language and anything and everything Spanish.

The other side did not play a fairer game. Spanish PP government officers in Madrid had no qualms about boosting outmoded and even archaic policing models, which have opened a revolving door to countless corruption cases, ranging from bribery to embezzlement, in most of the autonomous communities, including Catalonia. Central government offices at

veg fyrir atkvæði 750.000 manns vegna lögreglustöðvunar kjörseðla, samkvæmt tölum frá sjálfstjórnarhéraðinu Centralitarian Generalitat í Barcelona.

Auðvitað ætti Katalónska ríkisstjórnin að hafa skipulagt lagalegan þjóðaratkvæðagreiðslu og ekki sorglegt málamiðlun hlaupa síðastliðið 1-0 sem leiddi til alvarlegra öryggisáhættu frá upphafi og hafði jafnvel verið metin áður sem "*stórslys*" bæði borgarstjóra Madrid og Barcelona, Manuela Carmena og Ada Colau, í sjónvarpsviðtali fyrir nokkrum vikum. The Generalitat vísvitandi Pole-vaulted pólitískum stjórnarskránni sem þeir höfðu rætt um, samþykkt, samþykkt og undirritaður við Spáni árið 1978 eftir að herforingja Gen Francisco Franco lýkur, með það fyrir augum að endurlífga frestað sjálfstrausts drottningar í Katalónska kosningabaráttunni sem alin upp með sjálfstjórn menntastefnu sem, til þessa dags, hvetja til sveigjanlegra staðbundinna tilfinninga gegn ríkinu, tungumáli og öllu og öllu spænsku.

Hinum megin spilaði ekki sanngjarnari leik. Spænskir stjórnvöld í Spáni í Madrid höfðu enga áhyggjur í því að hrópa á óviðjafnanlegum og jafnvel fornleifafyrirtækjum sem hafa opnað snúnings dyr að ótal málum um spillingu, allt frá að múga til fjársviks í flestum sjálfstæðum samfélögum, þar á meðal

samo vlastito pravo na izbor, ostavivši za sobom više od 800 ozlijeđenih i spriječivši glasovanje 750 000 ljudi zbog policijske zapljene glasačkih kutija, prema podacima iz Generalitata, središnjeg tijela autonomne vlade u Barceloni.

Naravno da je katalonska vlada bila dužna organizirati legalan referendum, a ne tragičnu predstavu 1-0, što je od samog početka uzrokovalo ozbiljne sigurnosne rizike, te je čak i prije ostvarenja bilo proglašavano "katastrofom", od strane gradonačelnica Madrida i Barcelone, Manuele Carmena i Ade Colau, tijekom televizijskog intervjua prije nekoliko tjedana. Generalitat je namjerno preskočio politički Ustav o kojem su debatirali, kojega su prihvatili, odobrili i potpisali sa Španjolskom 1978. nakon završetka vojne diktature generala Francisca Franca, s namjerom oživljavanja odgođenih snova o neovisnosti u katalonskom elektoratu zasnovanom na samoodređenoj obrazovnoj politici koja, do dana današnjeg, potiče zatrovane lokalne osjećaje protiv države, jezika te svega živoga španjolskoga. Druga strana nije bila nimalo poštenija. Španjolski dužnosnici Narodne stranke u Madridu su se bez oklijevanja razmetali staromodnim, pa čak i arhaičnim modelima policijskog ponašanja, koja su otvorila začarani krug bezbrojnih slučajeva korupcije, od mita do pronevjere, u većini autonomnih zajednica, uključujući Kataloniju.

rido sonados casos del mismo estilo. El Estado español también tiene un redomado récord histórico de sordera a las peticiones de independencia que le ha hecho históricamente Cataluña, que devuelve con creces la moneda con una inflexibilidad férrea que siempre ha echado por tierra cualquier posibilidad de negociación.

Tuve que emigrar a Londres empujado por la crisis económica pero, habiendo vivido media vida allí, he formado y dejado buenos amigos catalanes, españoles y extranjeros en Barcelona; qué duda cabe. Son para quien viene de fuera la familia que escoge, y uno no se queda a vivir casi quince años sin interrupción en una tierra hostil. Sin embargo, muchos catalanes de a pie no (me) escuchan. Y, válgame la redundancia, de hablar ya ni hablamos, porque del sambenito de *"estos extranjeros nacionalizados que se pasan la vida riéndole las gracias a España (sic)"*, algunos no me dejan pasar. Lo bueno de este menosprecio es que es bastante democrático: mal puedo tomármelo personal, porque tampoco escuchan a los españoles, y ni entre ellos mismos se escuchan, prefiriendo vociferar lo que piensan sin perder el tiempo en escuchar, menos dejar hablar, al interlocutor. Y menos aún si éste es español y se siente catalán, mayormente por haber nacido allí y/o por haber pasado largas temporadas fuera del país: hoy, el fanatismo extremista ha hecho a este interlocutor invisible y le exige ser mudo. Es una

Palacio de la Moncloa have a track record of thorough deafness to the repeated demands for autonomy leading to independence from Catalonia, which is returning the treatment with the iron inflexibility that has always ruined any possibility of negotiation.

All this turmoil has driven many Catalans at street level to not listen to — not to mention engage in dialogue with — divergent voices. If you happen to be one of *"these nationalised foreigners who spend their lives laughing at anything Spain does or says"*, like yours truly, some may not even let you talk beyond the checkpoint. The good thing about this contempt is that it is quite democratic: I can hardly take it personally because they do not listen to Spaniards either, nor do they listen to each other, preferring to shout their thoughts without wasting time listening, let alone talking, to any interlocutor. It gets worse if he is Spanish and feels Catalan too, mainly because of having been born there and/or spending long periods abroad: today extremist fanaticism has made this interlocutor invisible and requires him to be mute. And that's a shame, because this last does listen to me, debates points and shows *seny* (a form of ancestral Catalan wisdom or sensibleness), neither winning nor losing an argument. This conversational partner only enriches their intellect and wants to build with ideas rather

Katalóníu. Ríkisstjórnin á Palacio de la Moncloa hefur afrekaskrá um ítarlegar heyrnarleysi við endurteknar kröfur um sjálfstæði sem eru í átt að sjálfstæði frá Katalóníu, sem er að koma aftur á meðferð með óstöðugleika í járni sem hefur alltaf eyðilagt alla möguleika á samningaviðræðum.

Allt þetta óróa hefur rekið marga katalöna á götuþrepi til að hlusta ekki — ekki sé minnst á að tala við — mismunandi raddir. Ef þú skyldir vera einn af "þessum þjóðernishömlu útlendingum sem eyða lífi sínu að hlæja eitthvað sem Spánn gerir eða segir", eins og sannarlega, gætu sumir ekki einu sinni látið þig tala utan við eftirlitsstöð. The góður hlutur óður í þetta fyrirlitning er að það er alveg lýðræðislegt: Ég get varla tekið það persónulega vegna þess að þeir hlusta ekki á Spánverja heldur hlustar ekki á hvort annað, frekar að hrópa hugsanir sínar án þess að eyða tíma í að hlusta, hvað þá að tala, við hvaða samtali. Það versnar ef hann er spænskur og finnur einnig katalónska, aðallega vegna þess að hann hefur verið fæddur þarna eða lengi lengi í útlöndum: í dag hefur öfgafullur ofstækismaður gert þessa samtali ósýnilega og krefst þess að hann sé óvirkur. Og það er synd, vegna þess að þessi síðasti hlustar á mig, umræður benda á og sýnir kynlíf (form af forfeðrandi kænsku speki eða skynfærni), hvorki að vinna né missa

Uredi Centralne vlade u zgradi Palacio de la Moncloa imaju povijest posvemašnje gluhoće ka ponavljanim katalonskim zahtjevima za autonomijom koja stremi ka neovisnosti, a koja sada uzvraća tretman sa željeznom nesavitljivošću i neprilagodljivošću kojom od samog početka uništava sve mogućnosti pregovora.

Sva ova previranja su natjerala mnoge Katalonce na ulici da jednostavno prestanu slušati – a kamoli govoriti – ustaničkim glasovima. Ako ste slučajno jedan on "*onih nacionaliziranih stranaca koji se čitav život smiju svemu što Španjolska učini ili kaže*", poput ovdje potpisanoga, neki vam neće dozvoliti čak ni da otvorite temu. Dobra stvar u ovom prijeziru jeste da je poprilično demokratičan: teško mi je shvatiti to osobno jer ni Katalonci ne slušaju Španjolce, nego jednostavno radije izvikuju vlastite misli bez gubljenja vremena na slušanje, a kamoli razgovor, sa jednakopravnim sugovornikom. Ako je taj nesretnik slučajno Španjolac, a osjeća se i Kataloncem, tad stvari postaju još gore, većinom zato što je rođen tamo i /ili je proveo mnogo vremena izvan zemlje: današnji ekstremistički fanatizam je ovog sugovornika učinio nevidljivim i zahtijeva od njega da bude nijem. To je zaista šteta, jer me gore spomenuti sluša, raspravlja o iznesenim primjedbama i pokazuje *seny* (oblik drevne katalonske mudrosti ili

pena, porque éste sí que (me) escucha, debate puntos y hace gala de 'seny' porque no gana ni pierde una discusión. Solo enriquece su intelecto y desea construir con sus ideas, más allá de satisfacer una pasión.

Un diálogo en este estado de cosas se hace una tarea monumental, y sin embargo, es lo único que puede volver al cauce la polarización política de la Cataluña post 1-0. No ha habido una campaña donde se interpele al conjunto de los catalanes, donde no se llame peyorativamente de *"espanyol"* al que no quiere independencia y donde todo el mundo se explique, razone o debata; sólo hay gritos y confusión, y desde el domingo también hay sangre. Es preciso desinfectar de odio y limpiar de cerumen la discusión catalana en los dos bandos; en vez de ir a las manos y a las caras, hay que abrir los brazos, dejar caer las porras y recibir al hermano.

Oye; si estás de acuerdo únete y si no lo estás propón alternativas, pero lo importante, lo altruista y humano, es que tenemos que hablar. *Q*

than satisfy passions.

A dialogue in this state of affairs has become a monumental task and, yet, it is the only thing that can undo the political polarisation of Catalonia post 1-O. There has not been a campaign where all the Catalans are asked for their opinion, where *"espanyol"* is not an insult to those who do not want independence, and where everyone explains, reasons or debates freely; there is only shouting and chaos, and since 1-O there is also blood. A disinfection of the hatred and a clearing of the earwax in the Catalan discussion from both sides is desperately needed; instead of using your hands you must open your arms, drop your batons and embrace your brother.

Hey, if you agree, join me and if you don't, propose an alternative. What is important, altruistic and human, is that we need to talk. *Q*

rök. Þessi samtalaaðili auðgar aðeins vitsmuni sína og vill byggja upp hugmyndir frekar en að fullnægja ástríðu.

Samtal í þessu máli hefur orðið stórfenglegt verkefni og þó er það eina sem getur afturkallað pólitíska fjölgun Katalóníu eftir 1-0. Það hefur ekki verið herferð þar sem allir katalönsku eru beðnir um skoðun þeirra, þar sem "*espanyol*" er ekki móðgun fyrir þá vilja ekki sjálfstæði og þar sem allir útskýra, rökstyðja eða ræða frjálslega. Það er aðeins að hrópa og óreiðu, og síðan 1-0 er einnig blóð. Sótthreinsun haturs og hreinsunar eyrnakrems í kænsku umræðu frá báðum hliðum er óþörf. Í stað þess að nota hendurnar þarftu að opna handlegg, sleppa batons og faðma bróður þinn.

Hæ, ef þú ert sammála að taka þátt í mér og ef þú leggur ekki til val. Það sem skiptir máli, altruistic og mannlegt, er að við verðum að tala. Q

razumnosti), bez pobjede ili poraza u raspravi. Ovaj sugovornik ne samo da obogaćuje njihov intelekt, nego želi i napredovati uz pomoć ideja, a ne samo zadovoljavati strasti.

Dijalog u ovakvom stanju stvari je postao monumentalna zadaća, a ujedno je i jedini čin koji može poništiti političku polarizaciju Katalonije nakon 1-0. Još se nije povela kampanja u kojoj se sve Katalonce pitalo za njihovo mišljenje, u kojoj "*espanyol*" nije uvreda onima koji ne žele neovisnost, u kojoj svi slobodno objašnjavaju, raspravljaju i debatiraju; postoje samo vika i kaos, a nakon 1-O postoji i prolivena krv. Očajnički nam treba raskuženje mržnje i ispiranje ušiju u katalonskoj diskusiji za obje strane; umjesto stiskanja šaka, morate baciti pendreke, otvoriti ruke i zagrliti svoga brata. Hej, ako se slažete, pridružite mi se, a ako ne, predložite drugo rješenje. Ono što je bitno, altruistično i ljudski, jeste činjenica da moramo razgovarati. Q

u nevremenu

završilo je vrijeme vedrih pjesama
vraćam se otamo odakle sam i krenula
iz čvorišta gorkog mraza, mrazne brade
i blatnog snijega od kojeg snjegovići ne rastu
a sanjke se ne troše
nema tu nikakvog pupoljka koji bi se
stezao u šaci filmskog mrtvaca
samoća je prenapučenost
množina stvari koje ti hropću za vratom
množina stvari, stare krame
koja iskrsava iz tame tavana
u mrskome klupku
pa ga ti odvezuj
taj mraz koji nije odveziv
taj snijeg koji nije otopiv
tu bradu koja se ceri
u gluhu noć
završilo je vrijeme vedrih pjesama

— *Evelina Rudan*

in bad weather

the time of sunny poems is finished
I go back to where I started from
from the knot of bitter frost, frosty beard
and muddy snow that grows no snowmen
and wears no sleighs down
nor is there a bud squeezed
in the film dead's fist
loneliness is overcrowding
the plurality of things that breathe at your neck
the plurality of things, the old junk
emerging from darkness in an attic
in a hateful yarn ball
now go try to untangle it
that frost that untangles not
that snow that melts not
that beard that grins
into the dead of night
the time of sunny poems is finished

— *Evelina Rudan*
(Tr. fr. the Croatian, Boris Gregorić)

en mal tiempo

la hora de poemas asoleados se acabó
vuelvo al lugar desde donde empecé
desde el amargo nudo helado, barba helada
y nieve lodosa en la que no crecen monos de nieve
y no se cansan ningunos trineos
ni hay un capullo apretado
en el puño del muerto en la película
la soledad es sobrepoblada por
la pluralidad de las cosas que respiran a tu cuello
la pluralidad de las cosas, trastos viejos
emergiendo de la oscuridad en un ático
en una odiosa bola de estambre
ahora ve y trata de desenredarla
esa escarcha que no desenreda
esa nieve que no se derrite
esa barba que sonríe
en lo muerto de la noche
la hora de poemas asoleados se acabó

— *Evelina Rudan*
(traducción, T. Warburton y Bajo y rvb)

bei schlechtem Wetter

die Zeit sonniger Gedichte ist vorbei
ich gehe zurück an den Ort, an dem ich begann
an den Knoten aus bitterer Kälte, kaltem Bart
und dreckigem Schnee, dem kein Schneemann entwächst
der keine Schlitten hinunterträgt
auch gibt es dort keine ausgepresste Knospe
in der Faust des Filmtoten
Einsamkeit wird übervölkert
die Vielheit von Dingen, die in deinem Nacken atmen
die Vielheit von Dingen, der alte Schrott
der aus dem Dunkel eines Estrichs auftaucht
in einem hasserfüllten Garnknäuel
nun geh und versuch es zu entwirren
diese Kälte, die sich nicht entwirrt
diesen Schnee, der nicht schmilzt
diesen Bart, der grinst
in den Tod der Nacht
die Zeit sonniger Gedichte ist vorbei

— *Evelina Rudan*
(nach dem Englischen von
Florian Vetsch)

Pjesma o junaku nježna srca i vedrih bradavica

Za junaka je najvažnije da ima
vedre bradavice i nježno srce.
Oboružan njima može osvojiti svijet
ili barem dvorište mojih susjeda.
To je dvorište na kraju svijeta,
tamo gdje se njiše lipov čaj
i palačinke s orasima,
suši se plahta, poplun i pelerina,
raste jelva, patuljak i mandarina,
kokoš je pristojne smeđe boje,
lastavica gradi gnijezdo,
auto gnječi suhu travu,
a susjed susjedu,
pa je junaku krajnje vrijeme da požuri.

— Evelina Rudan

The song about the hero with a gentle heart and bright nipples

For a hero, it's most important to have
bright nipples and a gentle heart.
Armed by these he can conquer the world
or at least my neighbor's yard.
It's the yard at the world's end,
there where the linden tea
and walnut crepes rock.
a sheet is drying, a comforter, a rain poncho,
a silver fir is growing, a dwarf and a tangerine,
a hen of decent gray color,
a swallow builds her nest,
a car presses against dried grass
just like a neighbor does to another
so it's high time for the hero to hurry up.

— Evelina Rudan
(Tr. fr. the Croatian, Boris Gregorić)

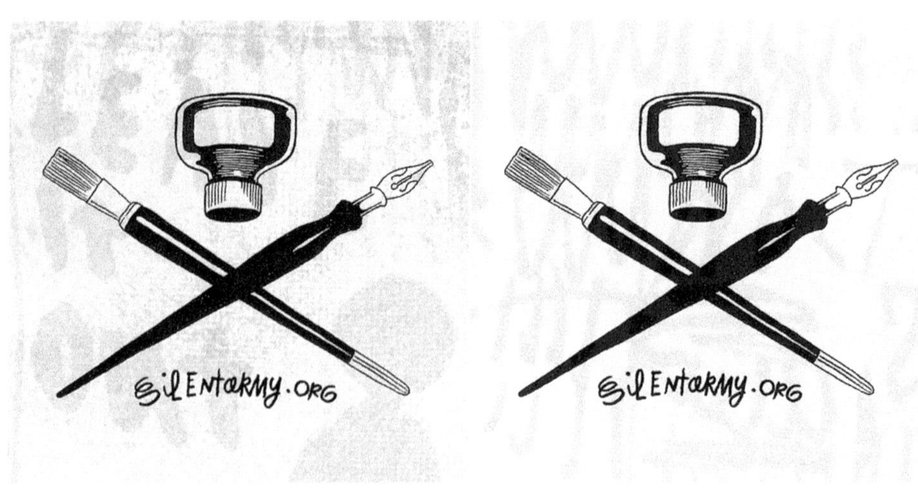

Canción acerca del héroe con corazón suave y pezones brillantes

Para un héroe lo más importante es tener
pezones brillantes y un corazón suave.
Armado con estos puede conquistar al mundo
o, al menos, al patio de mis vecinos.
Es el patio al fin del mundo,
allá donde el té de tilo
y crepas de nuez se mecen.
una sábana se está secando, una cobija, un poncho para la lluvia,
un abeto blanco está creciendo, un enano, un mandarino,
una gallina de color gris decente,
una golondrina construye su nido,
un coche presiona contra la hierba seca
como un vecino hace a otro
así que, es hora de que el héroe se dé prisa.

— *Evelina Rudan*
(traducción, T. Warburton y Bajo y rvb)

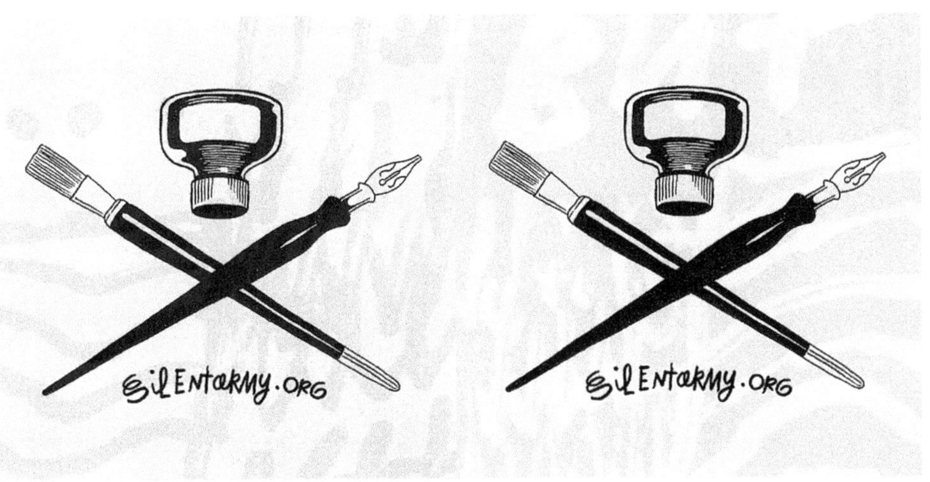

ikonų tapytojas

dar jauniklis būdamas,
jau žinojo: tapys ikonas

pusę gyvenimo meldėsi
pasninkavo

tapė ir degino

tapė ir degino

galų gale jam pavyko

o švenčiausia Madona,
šnabždėjo,
dusdamas iš padėkos ir iš
meilės
pilnomis akimis stebuklo

o tada jau pasiėmė tą paveikslą
ir
nesvarstydamas paliko namus,
ir išėjo į gatvės šurmulį

tuomet iškėlė tą vienintelį,
tą savo paveikslą ir nusilenkė
į visas keturias pasaulio puses

štai tuomet jį ir areštavo
pirmas pasitaikęs policininkas.
Už pornografijos platinimą.

— *Gintaras Grajauskas*

icon Painter

while yet a wee boy,
he knew: he'll paint icons

he prayed half his life
fasted

painted and burned it up

painted and burned it up

finally, he succeeded

O holiest Madonna, he whispered,
choking up from gratitude and love,
eyes filled with wonder

he took that picture, without
any thought — he left home
for the din of the streets

and he lifted up that one and only
picture of his, and bowed
to all four corners of the world

and was promptly arrested
by the first passing policeman
for the propagation of pornography

— *Gintauras Grajauskas*
(tr. fr. the Lithuanian,
Rimas Uzgiris)

Иконописец

pintor de iconos

aún sí´ndo un niño pequeñito,
él sabía: aba a pintar iconos

rezó la mitad de su vida
ayunaó

pintaba y lo quemó

pintaba y lo quemó

finalmente, tuvo éxito

ah santa virgen, susurró,
ahogándose de gratitud y amor,
ojos llenos de asombro

tomó esa pintura, sin pensarlo —
salió de casa

para el ruido de las calles

y levantó élsa única i solitaria
pintur sya, y se enclinó
hacia todas las cuatro esquinas del mundo

y fue prontamente arrestado
por el primer policía que pasaba
por propagación de pornografía

— Gintaras Grajauskas (traducción, T. Warburton y Bajo y rvb)

еще маленьким мальчиком
он уже знал, что будет писать иконы

он молился полжизни
постился

рисовал и сжигал

рисовал и сжигал

наконец, у него получилось

О, святая Мадонна, прошептал он,
задыхаясь от благодарности и любви,
глаза наполнились изумлением

и взял этот образ, без
какой-либо мысли, он вышел из дома
на шумные улицы

и, подняв вверх образ,
кланялся на каждом
из четырех углов мира

и был арестован
первым же проезжавшим полицейским
за распространение порнографии

— Гинтарас Гражаускас (перевóд, Андрей Сен-Сеньков)

Slikar ikona

dok je još bio maleni dječak,
znao je: slikat će ikone

molio se pola svog života
postio

slikao i spaljivao

slikao i spaljivao

konačno je uspio

O najsvetija Bogorodice, šapnuo je
grcajući od zahvalnosti i ljubavi
očiju prepunih čuda

uzeo je tu sliku, bez
ikakvih misli — napustio je dom

radi ulične vreve

i podigao je tu jednu i jednu
svoju sliku, naklonio se
svim četirima krajevima svijeta

uskoro ga je uhitio
prvi policajac u prolazu
zbog promicanja pornografije

— Gintaras Grajauskas (prijevod, Jelena Pataki)

kas
yra
interneto
centre

mistikai sako:
interneto centre tupi voras

netiesa netupi

sako profiai

tai tik didžiausias
pasaulio šiukšlynas
pilnas benamių
su naršyklėmis

įdomiausia jog internetas
yra Niekur

mes ten turime
savo adresus

— *Gintaras Grajauskas*

what
there
is
at
the
internet's
core

mystics say a spider squats
at the internet's core

no, say the specialists

he doesn't squat
but really, it's the biggest
garbage dump in the world
full of homeless people
with browsers

what's most fascinating is that
the internet is nowhere

and that's where we have
our addresses

— *Gintaras Grajauskas*
(tr. fr. the Lithuanian,
Rimas Uzgiris)

lo
que
hay
en
el
núcleo
de
internet

los místicos dicen que una araña se agacha
en el núcleo del internet

no, dicen los especialistas

no se agacha
pero realmente, es el más grande
vertedero de basura en el mundo
lleno de gente sin hogar
con navegadores del web

lo más fascinante es que
el Internet no está en ninguna parte

y allí es donde tenemos
nuestras direcciones

— *Gintaras Grajauskas*
(traducción, T. Warburton y Bajo y rvb)

Što
se
nalazi
u
jezgri
interneta

mistici kažu da pauk čuči
u jezgri interneta

ne, kažu specijalisti

ne čuči on tamo
ali zaista, to je najveće
odlagalište smeća na svijetu
puno beskućnika
sa pretraživačima

najviše pak fascinira to da
internet nije nigdje

a baš tamo se nalaze
naše adrese

— *Gintaras Grajauskas*
(prijevod s engleskoga, Ana Katana)

On that couch in the yard, at the edge of adulthood

On that couch in the yard, at the edge of adulthood,
you told me that falling is the laziest way to gain admiration.

Still we tried to catch stars with our outstretched hands,
children making grown up plans and

I swear I am trying to be brave but it's February, and the city is
shaking off snow like the sweat from a wet dream, sap crackling

like clotted honey in the trees' yawning veins, so I take two shots
of whiskey at the corner dive bar. The scars, like stars, fade

in early dusk. Bring me your back bent double with lonely. I'll
show you my tongue full of knots. I am tired of being

a mirror when you are looking for a window.
Please, won't you teach me how to open?

— *Brenda Taulbee*

Na kauču u dvorištu, na samom rubu odraslosti

Na kauču u dvorištu, na samom rubu odraslosti,
rekao si mi da samo lijeni padom pokušavaju pobuditi divljenje.

Ipak smo pokušavali uloviti zvijezde pruženim rukama,
tek djeca koja kuju odrasle planove, i

kunem ti se da pokušavam biti hrabra, ali veljača je i grad
otresa snijeg sa sebe kao znoj nakon mokrog sna, a smola pucketa

poput tučenoga meda u razjapljenim venama drveća, pa naručujem
dva viskija u birtiji na uglu. Ožiljci, poput zvijezda, blijede

u ranom sumraku. Donesi mi svoja leđa presavinuta od samoće. Ja
ću ti pokazati svoj jezik zavezan na čvorove. Ne želim više biti

zrcalo jer je prozor ono što ti želiš.
Molim te, bi li mi pokazao kako da se otvorim?

— *Brenda Taulbee*
(Prijevod, Ana Katana)

En aquel sofá en el patio, al borde de la adultez

En aquel sofá en el patio, al borde de la adultez,
me dijiste que caérse es la manera más perezosa de ganar la admiración.

Y aún así tratamos de atrapar estrellas con nuestras manos extendidas,
niños haciendo proyectos de adulto y

te juro que estoy tratando de ser valiente pero es Febrero, y la ciudad
se sacude la nieve, como sudor de un sueño húmedo, savia crepitante

como miel coagulada en las venas bostezantez de los árboles, así que tomo dos tragos
de whisky en la taberna de la esquina. Las cicatrices, como las estrellas, se desvanecen

a principios del crepúsculo. Tráeme tu espalda redoblada con la soledad. Te
mostraré mi lengua llena de nudos. Estoy cansada de ser

espejo cuando estás buscando una ventana.
Por favor, ¿enseñame como abrir?

— *Brenda Taulbee*
(traducción, T. Warburton y Bajo y rvb)

На этом диване во дворе, на краю взрослой жизни

На этом диване во дворе, на краю взрослой жизни,
ты сказал, что падение — самый легкий способ, чтобы тобой восхитились.

Еще мы, вытянув руки, пытались ловить звезды и строили планы, и,

клянусь, я пытаюсь быть храброй, но сейчас февраль, и город
стряхивает снег как пот с влажного сна, смола трескается

как запекшийся мед на деревьях зияющих вен, поэтому я беру два
стаканчика виски в забегаловке на углу. Шрамы, как звезды, исчезают

в ранних сумерках. Принеси, согнувшись в три погибели, одиночество. Я
покажу свой узловатый язык. Я устала быть

зеркалом, когда ты смотришь в окно.
Пожалуйста, научите меня открывать его.

— Бренда Толби
(перевóд, Андрей Сен-Сеньков)

How to choose the perfect avocado

Last year you tried to teach me
how to choose the perfect avocado.

"See?" you said, twisting off the hardened
knot of stem to check the fruit for readiness.

I still scour the produce department for evidence
you may have left. I want to tell you some habits

don't come easy.

I want to tell you I am still wrong more
often than I am right and I still

fill my mouth with the brown and rot of this.
There are some lessons you can't learn or teach.

When the fruit is ripe, I eat.

— *Brenda Taulbee*

Odabrati savršen avokado

Prošle godine si me pokušao naučiti
kako odabrati savršen avokado.

"Vidiš?" rekao si, vrteći otvrdnutu
stabljiku da provjeriš je li voćka zrela.

Ja još uvijek prekapam po voću i povrću tražeći dokaze
koje si možda ostavio. Želim ti reći da se neke navike

ne daju lako steći.

Želim ti reći da još uvijek češće pogriješim
nego što pogodim i još uvijek su mi
usta puna smeđega i truleži.
Neke lekcije se ne daju učiti i naučiti.

Kad voćka dozrije, ja jednostavno jedem.

— Brenda Taulbee
(Prijevod, Ana Katana)

Cómo escoger el aguacate perfecto

El año pasado trataste de enseñarme
cómo escoger el aguacate perfecto.

"¿ves?", dijiste, torciendo el nudo endurecido
del tallo para examinar la madurez de la fruta.

Todavía rebusco el departamento de verduras por evidencias
que puedes haber dejado. Quiero decirte que algunos hábitos

no vienen fácil.

Quiero decirte que aun estoy equivocado más
veces de la que estoy en lo cierto y que todavía me

lleno la boca con la marrón y putrefacta certeza de esto.
Hay algunas lecciones que no puedes aprender o enseñar.

Cuando la fruta está madura, yo como.

— *Brenda Taulbee*
(traducción, T. Warburton y Bajo y rvb)

Как выбрать идеальное авокадо

В прошлом году ты пытался научить меня
выбирать идеальное авокадо.

“Видишь?” — спрашивал ты, расплетая скрученный
в узел стебель, проверяя тем самым фрукт на зрелость.

Я до сих пор оттираю в овощном отделе улики, которые
ты, возможно, оставил. Хочется рассказать вам о некоторых привычках,

а это не так уж просто.

Хочется сказать вам, я все-таки чаще ошибаюсь
и мой рот до сих пор

наполнен чем-то коричневым и сгнившим.
Есть то, чему вы не можете научиться или научить.

Когда фрукт созрел, я просто его ем.

— Бренда Толби
(перевóд, Андрей Сен-Сеньков)

Knut Van Brijs,
Tradition/Traditie/традиција, *bricolage* (2017)

www.ingramcontent.com/pod-product-compliance
Ingram Content Group UK Ltd.
Pitfield, Milton Keynes, MK11 3LW, UK
UKHW020423250726
13967UKWH00007B/2786

Gobshite Quarterly

Double Trouble / Issue 30 – Spring 2018

This issue is dedicated to the memory of:

John Ashbery (28 July, 1927 — 3 Sept., 2017)
Holger Czukay (24 Mar., 1938 — 5 Sept., 2017)
Kate Millett (14 Sept., 1934 — 6 Sept., 2017)
Toshihiko Nakajima (中嶋 聡彦) (12 Aug., 1962 — 8 Sept., 2017)
J.P. Donleavy (23 Apr., 1926 — 11 Sept., 2017)
Sir Peter Hall (CBE) (22 Nov., 1930 — 11 Sept., 2017)
Grant Hart (18 Mar., 1961 — 13 Sept., 2017)
Harry Dean Stanton (14 July, 1926 — 15 Sept., 2017)
Kit Reed (7 June, 1932 — 24 Sept., 2017)
Danielle Darrieux (1 May, 1917 — 17 Oct., 2017)

12.00 USDOL || € 8.03462 EURO || £ 6.36 GBP (UK) || $ 12.0281 AUD (Oz) || $11.4795 CAN || ¥ 1,179.53 JPY (japan yen) || 115.380 SAR (S. Africa)

12.00 USDOL || € 8.03462 EURO || £ 6.36 GBP (UK) || $ 12.0281 AUD (Oz) || $11.4795 CAN || ¥ 1,179.53 JPY (japan yen) || 115.380 SAR (S. Africa)

This issue is dedicated to the memory of:

Olive Yang (楊金秀) a.k.a., Yáng Jīnxiù; Miss Hairy Legs (24 June, 1927 — 13 July, 2017)
Martin Landau (20 June, 1928 — 15 July, 2017)
John Heard (7 Mar., 1946 — 21 July, 2017)
Sam Shepard (5 Nov., 1943 — 27 July, 2017)
Brian Aldiss (18 Aug., 1925 — 19 Aug., 2017)
Dick Gregory (12 Oct., 1932 — 19 Aug., 2017)
John Abercrombie (16 Dec., 1944 — 22 Aug., 2017)
Jeannie Rousseau (1 Apr., 1919 — 23 Aug., 2017)
Mireille Darc (15 May, 1938 — 28 Aug., 2017)

Gobshite Quarterly

Double Trouble / Issue 29 – Winter 2018

Gobshite Quarterly

Double Trouble / Issue 30 – Spring 2018

photo, Benediktus Januševičius, Tekstai TV

Frequent GobQ contributor Tomica Bajsić, appearing at Poetinis Druskininkų ruduo 2017, 7 Oct., in Lithuania, as a part of Versopolis' European poetry platform.

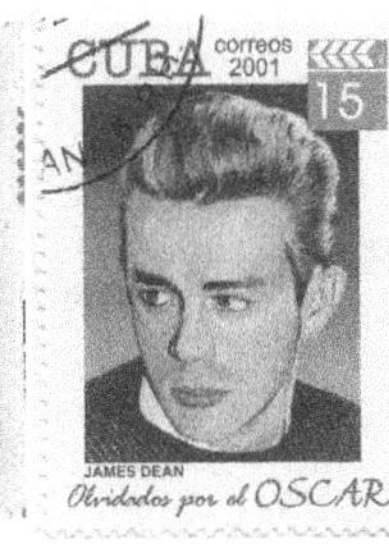

The Usual Suspects
Staff

Editor R. V. Branham

Office Mgr. Sofia Sensei Satori Shostakovna Satyagraha Stolicniya Sashimi Shitkicker

Assoc. Editor T. Warburton y Bajo

Contrib. Editors T. Warburton y Bajo & Channing Dodson & M. F. McAuliffe & Michael Lohr & Douglas Spangle

Field Correspondent Michael Lohr

House Tr. T. Warburton y Bajo (Sp.), Miguel Caminhão (Portuguese), チャニング・ドッドソン (Japanese). Алекса Сигала & Андрей Сен-Сеньков (Russian), Ani Gjika (Albanian), Anggo Genorga (Tagalog), Michael Lohr (Scand.) & rvb (Sp., & select Eng.), & a cohort of Croatian & Lithuanian translators

Design T. Warburton y Bajo

House Spanish Copyediting Lyda Alvarez, M.F. McAuliffe

Cover Illo Graham K. Willoughby

Cover comix & phfoto illos & franking Miroslav Nemeth Wheeler & var Postal Services.

Photos (except as noted) M. F. McAuliffe, T. Warburton y Bajo

Layout T. Warburton y Bajo & R. V. Branham

Prod. Tools InDesign, Photoshop (occasionally, when functional), Gimp, Dreamscope

Tech Support Sam Ward

Additional Editorial & Design Asstance Douglas Spangle & M.F. McAuliffe

Legal Peter Shaver

Publisher GobQ LLC/Reprobate Books

Double Trouble Flipbook double Issues printed Nov. & May of ea. year.

Post-production printing Ingram Spark/Lightning Source

Also distributed & printed nationally & internationally through Ingram Spark/Lightning Source POD

Sold through independent bookstores & available through Ingram & amazon dot com & WWW dot GobshiteQuarterly dot com

P.R. P. H. Vazak

Gobshite Quarterly: Double Trouble, Nos. 29/30, Winter & Spring 2018

ISBN 978-1-63587-868-4

GobQ volunteers: Qualified candidates please send résumé to

GobQ. LLC, 338 NE Roth St., Portland, OR 97211, or to gobq@yahoo.com

60 НЕ ПИШИТЕ ПИСЬМА. ИХ ПОТОМ ЧИТАЮТ, *Андрей Сен-Сеньков;*
Don't Write Letters. They Are Read Afterwards, *tr. fr. the Russian, A. Morse & P. Golub;*
61 No escriba cartas. Son leídos despuéz, *traducción, T. Warburton y Bajo y rvb;*
Nemojte pisati pisma. Ona se čitaju kasnije, *prijevod, Dijana Jakovac;*
(стихотворе́ние)(pome)(poema)(pjesma (Russia / Россия)

62 Iconic / ikonische / икопа (2017), *Knut Van Brijs;*
(bricolage) (Ghent / Sarajevo)

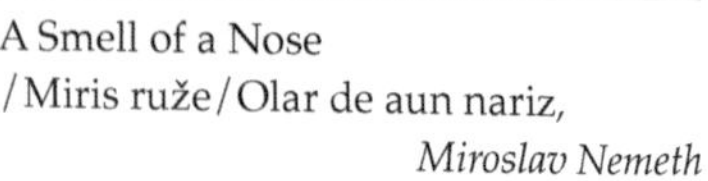

A Smell of a Nose
/ Miris ruže / Olar de aun nariz,
Miroslav Nemeth

Respectfully flip the book over, as Issue 29, Winter 2018, is a whole upsy-daisy 62 pgs away fr. the Spring 2018 issue

Gob Words

A word to give offense, when offense may be due. *Gobshite*, per OED, is what the American crew of Adm. Perry's Expedition to Japan were called by the natives; American Heritage Dictionary, 4th. ed., refers to a wad of expectorated chaw & to the Old Eng. *Shiten*; yet another dictionary refers to a Gobshite as a "*pernicious blatherskite*"—in other words, a stiff to read the teleprompter feed for CNN or for Rupert Murdoch's Fox "*News*" bullshit mountain & #FakeNews network. & as for those offended by the word, they can now be offended bilingually, trilingually, & quadrilingually, because all Eng. language pces have a foreign lang. *en-face* escort, whether Spanish, Arabic, Croatian, Icelandic, Farsi, Albanian, Finnish, Russian, Lithuanian, Gaelic, Japanese, Bangla, Punjabik &/ or whatever lang. is willing to put on its UN Observer cap. Wasn't it Pulitzer who said that journalism should comfort the afflicted & afflict the comfortable? Finally, we *are* a Rosetta Stone for the New World Order. — ***rvb***

The Usual Suspects
CONTRIBUTORS

Tomica Bajsić, a freq. *GobQ* contrib., based in Zagreb, Croatia, is an accomplished poet, essayist., tr. & journalist. Tomica returns w *Velika vrata rata/The Great Gates of War/Las Grandes Puertas de la Guerra/Didieji karo vartai (pjesma)(pome)(poema)(poezija)* (Crroat/Eng./Sp./Lith.). His books include *La Croix du Sud/So. Cross, Songs of Light & Shadow, & Amazona Diše*, a bilingual 2016 coll. of essays & pomes about his travels through the Amazon. A trilingual Croat/Eng./Sp. Reprobate coll. of his pomes is being planned for pub. in 2018.

Parantap Chakraborty is founder of Independent Press Birutjatio, based in Santiniketan, India, & teaches @ Domkal Girls' College. He tr. betw. Bangla & Eng., & makes his *GobQ* debut w/ his Bangla/Benga tr. of J. Heller Levi's *Jane Staying (2)/Jane Quedándose (2)*, also tr. into Nepali. (Eng./Bangla/Nepali/Sp.)

Justina Deksnytė, a student @ Vilnuis U., provided the Lith. tr. of T. Bajsić's *Velika vrata rata/The Great Gates of War/Las Grandes Puertas de la Guerra/Didieji karo vartai (pjesma) (pome)(poema)(poezija)* (Croat/Eng./Sp./Lith.)

Jan Heller Levi is the author of 3 pome colls.: *Orphan* (2014), *Skyspeak* (2005), & *Once I Gazed at You in Wonder* (1999). She's also ed. of *A Muriel Rukeyser Reader*, & co-ed., w./ Sara Miles, of *Directed by Desire: The Collected Poems of June Jordan*. W./ her husband, Swiss novelist Christoph Keller, she ed. *We're On: A June Jordan Reader*, pub., Sept., 2017. She has been a Hunter College faculty memeber in N.Y.C. since 2001. Jan makes her *GobQ* debut w./ *Jane Staying (2)*, also tr. into Sp. as *Jane Quedándose (2)*, as well as Bangla & Punjabi.

Dijana Jakovac, living in Rijeka, Croatia, has an MA in Eng. & Croat. She returns to *GobQ* w/ her Croat tr. of L. Rainer's *This is not one of those stories/Þetta er ekki ein af þessum sögum/Esta no es una de esas historias/Ovo nije jedna od oni priča (essay)(ritgerð)(ensayo)(esej)* (Eng./Icel./Sp./Croat), & A. Сен-Сеньков's *НЕ ПИШИТЕ ПИСЬМА. ИХ ПОТОМ ЧИТАЮТ/Don't Write Letters. They Are Read Afterwards/No escriba cartas. Son leídos despuéz/Nemojte pisati pisma. Ona se čitaju kasnije (стихотворéние)(pome)(poema)(pjesma)* (Russ./Eng./Sp./Croat)

Ana Katana, Croatian-based tr., who's tr. 20 novels into Croatian, returns to *GobQ* w/ her Croatian tr. of S. Morera's *A seducción, de Sofia Coppola: La arquitectura del vacío/The Beguiling of Sofia Coppola: The architecture of the vacuum/„Općinjen" Sofije Coppole: Arhitektura vakuma (ensayo)(essay)(esej)* (Sp./Eng./Croat)

Michael Lohr, frequent *GobQ* contrib., returns w/an Icel. tr. of L. Rainer's *This is not one of those stories/Þetta er ekki ein af þessum sögum/Esta no es una de esas historias/Ovo nije jedna od oni priča (essay)(ritgerð)(ensayo)(esej)* (Eng./Icel./Sp./Croat)

Sergio Morera, contrib. to Barcelona-based *Transit: cine y otros desvíos*, as well as a freq. *GobQ contrib.*, returns w/ *A seducción, de Sofia Coppola: La arquitectura del vacío/The Beguiling of Sofia Coppola: The architecture of the vacuum/„Općinjen" Sofije Coppole: Arhitektura vakuma (ensayo)(essay) (esej)* (Sp./Eng./Croat)

Ainsley Morse & Peter Golub return to *GobQ* w/their Eng. tr. of A. Сен-Сеньков's *НЕ ПИШИТЕ ПИСЬМА. ИХ ПОТОМ ЧИТАЮТ/Don't Write Letters. They Are Read Afterwards/No escriba cartas. Son leídos despuéz/Nemojte pisati pisma. Ona se čitaju kasnije (стихотворéние)(pome)(poema)(pjesma)* (Russ./Eng./Sp./Croa.), & *СТРОИТЕЛЬСТВО В ЛУЖНИКАХ КОНЦЛАГЕРЯ KRAFTWERK/The Construction of the Kraftwerk Concentration Camp/La construcción del campo de concentración de Kraftwerk/Izgradnja Kraftwerkova koncentracijskog logorai (стихотворéние)(pome)(poema)(pjesma)* (Russ./Eng./Sp./Croat). Morse's focus has been on tr. 20th. & 21st. C. Russ. & post-Yugoslav lit. since 2006, & her Harvard dissertation is on unofficial Soviet-era lit. Golub, a writer & tr. living in S.F., has been in *Circumference, PEN America, & Playboy*; his tr. focuses on contemporary Russ. poets, & he has worked on several anthols. incl. Jacket 2's online proj., *The New Russian Poetry*.

Donna Marie Mukhia teaches Eng. lit. @ Salesian College, Siliguri, India. She tr. betw. Eng. & Nepali. She makes her *GobQ* debut w/ a Nepali tr. of J. Heller Levi's *Jane Staying (2)/Jane Quedándose (2)*, also tr. into

Bangla/Bengla. (Eng./Banglia/Nepali/Sp.)

Miroslav Nemeth, freq. *GobQ* contrib., & originating w/ Zagreb's Wild-Eyed comix collective, returns w/ a complete graphic novella, *A Smell of a Nose/Miris ruže/Olar de aun nariz (comix)* (Eng./Croat./Sp.)

Jelena Pitaki, Croat writer & tr., returns to *GobQ* w/her Croat tr. of M. Nemeth's *A Smell of a Nose/Miris ruže/Olar de aun nariz (comix)* (Eng./Croat./Sp.), &. of *A. Сен-Сеньков's СТРОИТЕЛЬСТВО В ЛУЖНИКАХ КОНЦЛАГЕРЯ KRAFTWERK/The Construction of the Kraftwerk Concentration Camp/La construcción del campo de concentración de Kraftwerk/Izgradnja Kraftwerkova koncentracijskog logorai (стихотворéние)(pome)(poema)(pjesma)*(Russ./Eng./Sp./Croat)

Leah Rainer, until recently, a Little Beirut-based poet & essayist, now resides in Albany, NY. For those who miss her, & for those discovering her for the first time, we offer *This is not one of those stories/Þetta er ekki ein af þessum sögum/Esta no es una de esas historias/Ovo nije jedna od oni priča (essay)(ritgerð) (ensayo)(esej)* (Eng./Icel./Sp./Croat)

Андрей Сен-Сеньков / Andrei Sen-Sekov, residing in Moscow, is author of 10+ books of pomes & prose, incl. *Anatomical Theater*, as well as Russ. tr. of pomes, & a children's book, *A Cat Named Mouse*. In the US, his work's been in *Aufgabe, Interim, & Jacket*, & the anthol., *Crossing Centuries*. His own orig. Russ. pomes, & his generous Russ. tr. of work by other *GobQ* contribs. have been feat. in recent issues. He returns w/ *СТРОИТЕЛЬСТВО В ЛУЖНИКАХ КОНЦЛАГЕРЯ KRAFTWERK/The Construction of the Kraftwerk Concentration Camp/La construcción del campo de concentración de Kraftwerk/Izgradnja Kraftwerkova koncentracijskog logorai (стихотворéние)(pome)(poema)(pjesma)*(Russ./Eng./Sp./Croat.), & *НЕ ПИШИТЕ ПИСЬМА. ИХ ПОТОМ ЧИТАЮТ/Don't Write Letters. They Are Read Afterwards/No escriba cartas. Son leídos despuéz/Nemojte pisati pisma. Ona se čitaju kasnije (стихотворéние)(pome)(poema) (pjesma)* (Russian/Eng./Sp./Croat).

Damir Šodan, born in 1964 in Split, Croatia, who's been a GobQ contrib. since 2002, returns w/an Eng. tr. of *Velika vrata rata/The Great Gates of War/Las Grandes Puertas de la Guerra/Didieji karo vartai (pjesma) (pome)(poema)(poezija)* (Croat/Eng./Sp./Lith.)

Knut Van Brijs, orig. fr. Ghent, but now residing in Sarejevo, makes his *GobQ* debut w/ *Iconic/ikonische/икона* (2017) (bricolage)

T. Warburton y Bajo y rvb did co-tr. of works by T. Bajsić , J. Heller Levi, M. Nemith, L. Rainer, & A. Сен-Сеньков into Span.; rvb's Eng. tr. of S. Morero's essay was commissioned for this issue.

Graham Willoughby, whose artwork's adorned our covers since the 2nd. is., returns, & still in watery colour! Graham has exhibited in galleries in the US, Germany & his native Oz, & has artist books in museum colls. worldwide.

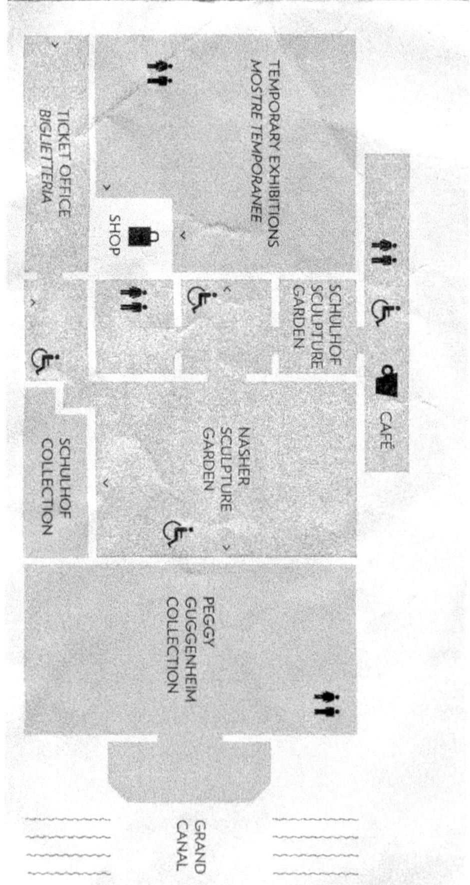

Velika vrata rata

Davoru Sefiću

Vozili smo 2000 km preko Europe
u "Golden boyu", starom Robijevom Kadettu.
Nas trojica,
pili smo, pušili i slušali radio,
duge strijele sunca na
mokroj cesti. Kilometri padaju

i noć se diže, stajemo samo
da se zamijenimo za volanom i idemo dalje.
Pijemo, pušimo i slušamo radio i
tako postaje dan. Nebo se širi.
Ti govoriš:
"40 godina, bar toliko, to je dovoljno dug život,
i ne treba mi više."

A nedugo zatim tenkovska granata kod Dubrovnika
odnijet će te u atmosferu, živio si 23 godine,
ne 40.

Prije sedam godina,
vozili smo bez stajanja 2000 km preko Europe
sve do četničke barikade na Plitvicama.
Bio je Uskrs i

ušli smo ravno na velika vrata rata.

Na jedinoj tvojoj fotografiji u uniformi
imaš začuđen pogled, kao da vidiš ispred.
Na zidu iza tebe je nekakva bijela svjetlost, koja
dolazi od Duha, i sveprisutna je.

— Tomica Bajsić

The Great Gates of War

(for Davor Sefić)

We drove 2,000 miles all across Europe
in our Golden Boy, Robi's old Kadett:
the three of us,
smoking, listening to the radio,
long arrows of light
stretched along the wet road. Miles pile behind us

and night emerges; we stop only
to change at the wheel, continuing on, breathlessly.
Drinking, smoking, listening to the radio
that's how we meet the daylight. The sky expands
and you're saying,
40 years, that's just about right. I don't need more,
that's long enough for one life.

Shortly afterward a tank grenade near Dubrovnik
will take you up into the atmosphere; you lived 23 years
instead of 40.

Seven years ago
we had driven relentlessly all across Europe
up to that Chetnik [1] roadblock at Plitvice.
It was Easter

and we passed through the Great Gates of War.

In your only photograph taken in uniform
you have a curious look, as if you can see what's coming ahead.
On the wall above you a flash of white light
coming from the Spirit — its everpresence.

— *Tomica Bajsić*
(Tr. fr. the Croatian, Damir Šodan)

[1] **Tanslator's note:** *Historically, Chetniks were Serbian self-styled monarchist elite military units established before W.W. I. During W.W. II, they sided with the fascists & fought against Tito's partisans. In the early 1990s, they resurfaced as right wing nationalist paramilitaries on a territory of former Yugoslavia fighting alongside the Jugoslav National Army in a war for Greater Serbia & are responsible for many atrocities during the aggresion on Croatia & Bosnia.* **(1991).**

Las grandes puertas de la guerra

(para Davor Sefić)

manejamos 2.000 millas toda Europa
en nuestro Golden Boy, el viejo Kadett de Robi:
tres de nosotros,
fumar, escuchando la radio,
largas flechas de luz
estiramiento a lo largo de la carretera mojada. A montenes millas detrás de nosotros

y emerge de la noche, sólo nos paramos
a cambiar en la rueda, continuando, sin aliento.
Beber, fumar, escuchar la radio
que es como encontramos con la luz del día. El cielo se expande
y estás diciendo,
40 años, eso es sólo de derecho. No necesito más,
es suficiente para una vida.

Poco después una granada de tanque cerca de Dubrovnik
le llevará la atmósfera, vivió 23 años
en lugar de 40.

Hace siete años
que habíamos conducido inexorablemente toda Europa
hasta eso Chetnik [1] barricada en Plitvice.
Era la pascua

y pasamos por las puertas grandes de guerra.

En su única fotografía tomada en uniforme
tienes una mirada curiosa, como si puede ver lo que viene delante.
En la pared por encima de ti un destello de luz blanca
que viene del espíritu — siempre presente.

— *Tomica Bajsić*
(traducción de la croata, T. Warburton y Bajo y rvb)

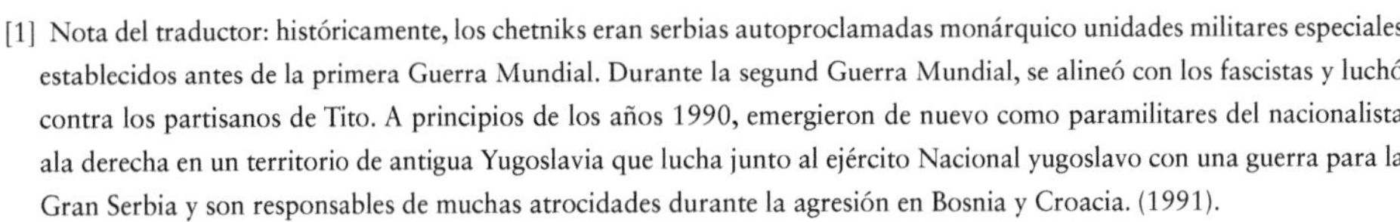
[1] Nota del traductor: históricamente, los chetniks eran serbias autoproclamadas monárquico unidades militares especiales establecidos antes de la primera Guerra Mundial. Durante la segund Guerra Mundial, se alineó con los fascistas y luchó contra los partisanos de Tito. A principios de los años 1990, emergieron de nuevo como paramilitares del nacionalista ala derecha en un territorio de antigua Yugoslavia que lucha junto al ejército Nacional yugoslavo con una guerra para la Gran Serbia y son responsables de muchas atrocidades durante la agresión en Bosnia y Croacia. (1991).

Didieji karo vartai

(skirta Davor Sefić)

Mes nuvažiavom 2000 kilometrų skersai Europos
mūsų „Golden Boy", senu Robio Kadett'u:
mes trise,
rūkėm, klausėm radijo,
ilgos šviesos strėlės
tįso šlapiame kelyje. Kilometrai lieka užnugary

ir išnyra naktis, mes stojam tik
pasikeisti prie vairo, ir judam toliau,
nepailstamai.
Gėrėm, rūkėm, klausėm radijo,
taip mes pasitikome dieną. Dangus driekiasi.
Tu sakai,
40 metų, maždaug tiek užtenka vienam gyvenimui,
man nereikia daugiau.

Netrukus po to tanko sviedinys netoli Dubrovniko
išmes tave aukštyn į atmosferą, tu gyvenai 23 metus,
ne 40.

Prieš septynis metus
mes nepaliaujamai važiavom skersai Europos
iki pat to četnikų užtvaros Plitvicoje.
Tada buvo Velykos

ir mes žengėme pro didžiuosius karo vartus.

Vieninteléje nuotraukoje su uniforma
tu žiūri nustebusiu žvilgsniu, tarsi matytum kas artėja.
Ant sienos virš tavęs yra balta šviesa, kuri
kyla iš Dvasios ir ji visur esanti.

— *Tomica Bajsić*
(iš anglų k. vertė, Justina Deksnytė)

jane, staying (2)

the doctors gave you four weeks
now we're going on six

in between, grace stopped eating and went into the
stars

you little mandelstam without a revolution
but I love this poor earth,
because I have not seen another

your hands loop in the air around your window chair,
around your window body

— *Jan Heller Levi*

জেন্ , থাকছে (২)

ডাক্তাররা তোমায় দিয়েছিল চার সপ্তাহ
এখন তোমার ছয় চলছে

এর মাঝে গ্রেস খাওয়া ছেড়ে দিয়েছে আর তারায় গেছে চলে

তুমি বিপ্লব ছাড়াই ছোট্ট ম্যান্ডেলষ্টাম
"কিন্তু আমি এই দীন পৃথিবীকেই ভালোবাসি
কারণ আমি আর একটাও দেখিনি"

তোমার জানলার ধারের চেয়ারের উপরে শূন্যে তোমার হাত
দুটো ঘুরছে,তোমার শরীর জানলার চারদিকে।

-জান হেলার লিভী

-ইংরেজী থেকে অনুবাদ: পরন্তপ চক্রবর্তী

Santiniketan/St. Gallen/Little Beirut

Jane, quedándose (2)

los doctores te dieron cuatro semanas
ahora vamos en seis

en medio, Grace dejó de comer y fue hacia las estrellas

tu pequeño Mandelstam sin una revolución
pero amo esta pobre tierra,
porque no he visto otro

sus manos ce cierran en el aire alrededor de tu silla de la ventana,
alrededor de tu cuerpo de ventana

— *Jan Heller Levi*
(traducción, T. Warburton y Bajo y rvb)

जेन बस्छे (२)

डाक्टरहरुले तिमीलाई चार हप्ता दिए
अब हामी लाग्दैछौं छ तिर बढ्न

बिचैमा ,ग्रेस खान छोडी गई तारा भ्रमण गर्न

इन्कलाब बिनाको तिमी एउटी सानी मन्देलस्तम्भ
"तर म माया गर्छु यो गरिब संसारलाई"
कारण अर्को देखिनं मैले"

तिम्रा हातहरु हावामा घुम्छन् झ्याल छेउका
कुर्सी वरि परि, झ्याल जस्तो शरीर तिम्रो त्यही वरि परि

—ज्यान हेल्लर लेवी

—— डन्ना मारी मुखियाद्वारा अंग्रेजीबाट अनुवादित

MIROSLAV NEMETH

A SMELL FROM A NOSE

Miris ruže

Olor de una nariz

Prerano sam se počeo osvrtati na svoj život

comencé a mirar hacia atrás en mi vida demasiado temprano

Sjećam se da me majka držala za ruku i vodila po cijelom gradu

recuerdo que mi madre me llevaba de la mano por toda la ciudad.

Djed me također vodio u šetnju po susjedstvu

mi abuelo también solía llevarme a dar un paseo por el barrio.

Moja obitelj živjela je u neboderu. Imao sam mnogo prijatelja i čuvam uspomene na to vrijeme.

mi familia vivía en un rascacielos. Tenía muchos amigos y guardo esos momentos en la memoria.

MY BROTHER AND I SHARED A ROOM WITH A NICE VIEW TO THE NORTH. WE COULD SEE THE TOWER ON THE TOP OF THE TOWNHILL.

Moj brat i ja dijelili smo sobu s lijepim pogledom na sjever. Mogli smo vidjeti toranj na vrhu gradskog brežuljka.

mi hermano y yo compartimos una habitación con una bonita vista al norte. Podiamos ver la torre en la cima de la colina de la ciudad.

Boris je uskoro postao Titov pionir na školskoj ceremoniji. Mahao sam malenom zastavom.

Boris pronto se convirtió en un pionero de Tito en una ceremonia escolar. Yo agitaba una banderita.

Nakon dvije godine i sâm sam krenuo u školu s drugom djecom pod toplim jutarnjim suncem.

dos años más tarde yo también comencé a ir a la escuela con otros niños, calentados por el sol matutino.

U djetinjstvu sam volio putovati automobilom, naročito tijekom dugih putovanja za praznike.

cuando niño me encantaba viajar en coche, especialmente largos viajes a vacaciones.

Volio sam sunce, more i nebo. Volio sam skakati u vodu.

me encantaba el sol, el mar y el cielo. Me encantaba saltar al agua.

U to sam vrijeme otkrio Boga. Primio me u svoje naručje te sam odlazio u crkvu.

en esa época descubrí a Dios. Me tomó en sus brazos y fui a la iglesia.

THE CROSS STILL STANDS ON THE CROSSROADS NEAR THE CHURCH, AS A REMINDER ON MY WAY HOME.

Križ još uvijek stoji na raskrižju blizu crkve, kao podsjetnik na moj put kući.

la cruz sigue en la encrucijada cerca de la iglesia, como un recordatorio en mi camino a casa.

Imao sam dar za nogomet. Provodio sam mnogo vremena na igralištu.

tenía talento para el fútbol. Solía pasar mucho tiempo en los campos de juego.

Ostajali bismo na igralištu do mraka. Ponekad bih ostao sasvim sam.

nos quedabamos en el patio hasta que oscurecía. A veces yo era el único que quedaba.

Na početku mojih tinejdžerskih godina preselili smo se u kuću blizu gradskog groblja.

al comienzo de mi período de adolescencia nos mudamos a una casa cerca del cemeterio de la ciudad.

Prvog studenoga svake godine rijeka bi ljudi prošla pokraj moje kuće na putu do groblja.

el 1° de noviembre de cada año un río de gente pasaba por mi casa en camino al cementario

ONE OF MY FIRST EXPERIENCES OF DEATH WAS WHEN I SAW MY GRANDMOTHER SLAUGHTERING THE CHICKEN IN THE BACKYARD OF HER HOUSE IN SUBURBIA.

Jedno od mojih prvih iskustava sa smrću bilo je ono kada sam vidio baku kako kolje kokoš u dvorištu svoje kuće u predgrađu.

una de mis primeras experiencias con la muerte fue cuando ví my abuela matando un pollo en el patio trasero de su casa en los suburbios

Shvatio sam da je život poput svijeće. U mene je ušao strah.

me di cuenta de que la vida es como una vela. Un miedo entró en mí.

Postao sam ovisan o svojoj kući. Jedva sam čekao da se vratim.

me volví adicto a mi casa. No podía esperar para volver a casa.

Kuća se poigravala mnome kao lutkom; nisam se žalio, volio sam trpjeti.

la casa jugaba conmigo como un títere;
No tenía ninguna queja, disfrutaba ser pasivo.

Slušao bih glasnu glazbu i trošio energiju na smiješne vježbe u svojoj sobi.

yo escuchaba música ruidosa y gastaba energía en ejercicios absurdos en mi habitación.

Odjednom sam otkrio grafičku umjetnost, idealan način da se otisnem.

de repente descubrí el arte gráfico, ideal para exprimirme.

Sanjao sam ružne snove poput toga da me netko čeka pred vratima moje sobe. Želio mi je nešto pokazati.

tenía unos sueños aterradores, como alguien esperándome en la puerta de mi habitación. Quería enseñarme algo.

Moja je seksualnost na kraju pronašla izričaj u nesvjesnom.

mi sexualidad eventualmente encontró expresión en la inconsciencia.

prijevod, Jelena Pataki

traducción, t. warburton y bajo y rwb

Noćna polucija raspršila je moje sjeme posvuda po kući, čak i u sobama za koje nisam znao da postoje, koje su čekale da ih otkrijem.

la contaminación nocturna dejó mi semilla por todas partes en la casa, incluso en las habitaciones que no sabía que existían, esperando a ser descubierta.

This is not one of those stories

Leah Rainer

I stood up from my bed, lost. My room was suddenly too big and too small at the same time and the floor was the only place that I felt able to exist. I clutched my body and let out a full-bellied yell. Certain it was a mistake, I picked up my phone to scroll through our last text conversation. We had just talked yesterday. The timing couldn't make sense. She had told me she had the flu. It was a regular conversation just like any other and it didn't make sense. Some time later, a friend sent me a link to the article that our local newspaper had published about her death. It had the most up to date reporting of the incident and it was sent to me with a warning that it was a graphic story.

I would be lying if I told you I hadn't ever imagined she might die too soon. She was the sort of friend who talked about death a lot. She lived in a basement and read a lot of Bukowski and would occasionally send me pictures of herself in the mirror in an unbuttoned flannel, a flat little stomach and a simple bra, with a caption saying "alco-

Þetta er ekki ein af þessum sögum

Leah Rainer

(þýtt úr Ensku, Michael Lohr)

Ég stóð upp úr rúminu mínu, missti. Herbergið mitt var skyndilega of stórt og of lítið á sama tíma og gólfið var eina staðurinn sem ég fannst geta verið til. Ég klúðraði líkama mínum og lék fullt bellied yell. Vissulega var það mistök, ég tók upp símann minn til að fletta í gegnum síðustu textasamtalið okkar. Við höfðum bara talað yester-daginn. Tímasetningin gat ekki skilið. Hún hafði sagt mér að hún hefði flensu. Það var venjulegur samantekt eins og allir aðrir og það var ekki skynsamlegt. Nokkru síðar sendi vinur mér tengil á greinina sem staðbundin dagblaðið okkar hafði gefið út um dauða hennar. Það hafði mest upp til dagsetning tilkynning um atvikið og það var sent til mín með viðvörun um að það væri grafísk saga.

Ég myndi ljúga ef ég sagði þér að ég hef aldrei hugsað mér að hún gæti dáið of fljótt. Hún var svona vinur sem talaði mikið um dauðann. Hún bjó í kjallara og las mikið af Bu-Kowski og sendi mér stundum myndir í speglinum í unbuttoned flannel, flatum litlum maga og einföldum brjóstahaldara, með yfirskriftinni sem segir að "alkóhólismi gerir líkamann góða.

Esta no es una de esas historias

Leah Rainer

(traducción, T Warburton y bajo y rvb)

Me levanté de mi cama, perdida. Mi cuarto era de repente demasiado grande y demasiado pequeño al mismo tiempo y el piso era el único lugar que yo sentí capás de existir. Agarré mi cuerpo y solté un grito lleno desde mi vientre. Segura de que era un error, cogí mi teléfono para repasar nuestra última conversación en texto. Acabábamos de hablar ayer. El tiempo no tenía sentido. Me había dicho que tenía gripe. Era una conversación normal, como cualquier otra y no tenía sentido. Algún tiempo después, un amigo me envió un enlace al artículo que nuestro periódico local había publicado acerca de su muerte. Era el reportaje con la información más actualizada del incidente y me fué enviado con la advertencia de que era una historia gráfica.

Te estaría mintiendo si yo te dijera que nunca me imaginé que ella podría morir demasiado pronto. Era el tipo de amiga que hablaba mucho acerca de la muerte. Vivía en un sótano y leía mucho a Bukowski y de vez en cuando me enviaba fotos de sí misma al espejo en una franela desabrochada, un pequeño estómago plano y un brasier simple, con una leyenda que decía: "el alcoholismo es bueno para el cuerpo".

Ovo nije jedna od oni priča

Leah Rainer

(prijevod, Dijana Jakovac)

Ustala sam iz kreveta, izgubljena. Moja je soba odjednom bila prevelika i premalena u isto vrijeme i pod je bio jedino mjesto gdje sam osjećala da postojim. Stisnula sam svoje tijelo i vrisnula iz dna duše. Sigurno se radilo o pogrešci, uzela sam mobitel kako bih pogledala naš posljednji tekstualni razgovor. Baš smo jučer razgovarale. Tajming nije odgovarao. Rekla mi je da ima gripu. Bio je to sasvim običan razgovor poput svakoga drugog pa sve to nije imalo smisla. Nešto kasnije, prijatelj mi je poslao link na članak u kojemu su naše lokalne novine objavile vijest o njezinoj smrti. Sadržavao ažurirano izvješće slučaja i poslan mi je s upozorenjem da se radi o grafičkom sadržaju.

Lagala bih vam kad bih rekla da nikada nisam zamišljala da bi ona mogla umrijeti prerano. Bila je tip prijatelja koji je mnogo govorio o smrti. Živjela je u podrumu i čitala mnogo Bukowskog i s vremena na vrijeme slala bi mi fotografije sebe u ogledalu u raskopčanom flanelu, s ravnim trbuščićem i u jednostavnom grudnjaku, s natpisom: „Alkoholizam je dobar za tijelo." Osjećala

holism does the body good." She was wracked with guilt about her student loan debt because her parents had co-signed and they already didn't have much. The way she saw it, with a Bachelors in English the only way out of the debt would be if she died. She was hopelessly in love with a straight girl with long dark hair who made pendants out of bullet casings and crystal points. For the amount she drank and talked about death, there are certain story lines that would have saddened me but which would not have surprised me.

This is not one of those stories.

The article began as most articles about dead people do. It recounted her accomplishments, acknowledged her family, and explained that she had just moved to New Orleans from our hometown only a few months ago. The man's name was Henry but he went by Hank and I'd tell you his last name but I never bothered to learn how to pronounce it. The picture of him was small but you could tell he was bulky with a swollen brow. He was black, and I wouldn't tell you that except that it's relevant because police response rates to domestic abuse calls in black neighborhoods in New Orleans are significantly lower than their response rates to the same sort of calls in white neighborhoods and maybe if they had shown up one of those times his ex-girlfriend called them, I wouldn't be writing this sto-

"Hún var slegin með sektarkennd um skuldir nemenda lánveitunnar vegna þess að foreldrar hennar höfðu undirritað og þeir höfðu ekki mikið. Hvernig hún sá það, með bachelor á ensku, eina leiðin út úr skuldinni væri ef hún dó. Hún var vonlaust ástfanginn af beinni stúlku með langa dökku hári sem gerði pendants úr kúluhúð og crys-tal stigum. Fyrir þá upphæð sem hún drakk og talaði um dauða, þá eru ákveðnar sögulínur sem myndu hafa dapað mig en sem hefði ekki hissa á mig.

Þetta er ekki ein af þessum sögum.

Greinin hófst eins og flestir greinar um dauð fólk gera. Hún sagði frá henni, viðurkenndi fjölskyldu sína og útskýrði að hún hefði bara flutt til New Orleans frá heimabæ okkar fyrir nokkrum mánuðum. Maðurinn heitir Henry en hann fór með Hank og ég myndi segja þér eftirnafnið sitt en ég nenni aldrei að læra hvernig á að kenna það. Myndin af honum var lítill en þú gætir sagt að hann væri fyrirferðarmikill með bólginn brúnu. Hann var svartur og ég myndi ekki segja þér það nema að það sé viðeigandi vegna þess að svörun lögreglunnar til heimilisnotkunar símtala í svörtum hverfum í New Orleans eru verulega lægri en svörun þeirra við sömu símtöl í hvítum hverfum og kannski ef þeir hefðu sýnt einn af þeim tíma sem fyrrverandi kærastan hans kallaði þá, myndi ég ekki skrifa þessa sögu. Hank hafði glæsilega skrá, aðallega

Estaba atormentada por la culpa que sentía por su deuda estudiantil porque su padres habían firmado por ella, y ellos no tenían mucho. A su manera de ver las cosas, con un título universitario en inglés, la única manera de salir de deudas sería si ella muriera. Estaba enamorada sin esperanzas de una chica recta con cabello largo y oscuro que hacía collares con cartuchos de balas y puntas de cristal. Con la cantidad que ella bebia y hablaba de la muerte, hay ciertas líneas de la historia que me habrían entristecido, pero que no me han sorprendido.

Esta no es una de esas historias.

El artículo comenzó como la mayoría de los artículos sobre los muertos. Relató sus logros, reconoció a su familia y explicó que se acababa de trasladar a Nueva Orleans de nuestra ciudad natal hacía sólo pocos meses. El hombre se llamaba Henry, pero le decían Hank, y te diría su apellido pero nunca me molesté en aprender a pronunciarlo. La foto de él era pequeña, pero se veía que era voluminoso, con una ceja hinchada. Él era negro y yo no hubiera mencionado eso, excepto que es pertinente porque el número de respuestas de la policía a las llamadas de abusos domésticos en los barrios negros de Nueva Orleáns son significativamente inferiores al número de respuestas al mismo tipo de llamadas en barrios blancos, y tal vez si se hubieran presentado una de esas veces cuando su ex-novia les llamó, yo no estaría escribiendo esta historia. Hank tenía una ficha criminal impresionante, principalmente acusaciones por delitos de dro-

je grižnju zbog duga za studentski kredit jer su ga njezini roditelji supotpisali i već sada nisu imali dovoljno novaca. Kako je ona to vidjela, s prvostupanjskom diplomom iz engleskoga jezika, jedini način izlaska iz duga bio je da umre. Bila je beznadno zaljubljena u strejt djevojku duge tamne kose koja je izrađivala privjeske od čahura metaka i šiljastih kristala. Koliko je pila i govorila o smrti, sigurno ima priča koje bi me rastužile, ali koje me isto tako ne bi iznenadile.

Ovo nije jedna od takvih priča.

Članak je započeo kao što započinje većina članaka o mrtvima. Nabrajao je njezine uspjehe, izvijestio o njezinoj obitelji i ukazao na to da se ona nedavno preselila u New Orleans iz našega rodnog grada prije samo nekoliko mjeseci. Ime muškarca bilo je Henry, ali su ga zvali Hank i rekla bih vam njegovo prezime, ali se nikada nisam zamarala kako bi ga trebalo izgovarati. Fotografija njega je bila sićušna, ali se moglo vidjeti da je ogroman i natečena čela. Bio je Afroamerikanac, i ne bih vam bila to rekla da nije bilo iz razloga što su učestalosti odgovora policije na pozive o obiteljskom nasilju u afroameričkim četvrtima u New Orleansu značajno rjeđe od učestalosti odgovora na iste takve pozive u četvrtima bijelaca, i možda da su se pojavili samo jednom kada ih je njegova bivša djevojka bila zvala, ja ne bih bila pisala ovu priču. Hank je imao impresivan dosje, uglavnom su to bile optuž-

ry. Hank had an impressive record, mostly drug charges and grand larceny, one attempted murder charge that had been dropped in '93. He had spent his most recent stint in jail on charges involving heroin and had been released a week ago. His ex-girlfriend worked with Sarah at a restaurant and the two had been living together for a few weeks while Sarah was between places. The newspaper reported accounts from their co-workers saying that Hank would come by the restaurant most nights, drunk, threatening to kill his ex-girlfriend. No one took him very seriously, and maybe this night wasn't the first night he broke into the apartment but it was the first time anyone had been there.

She had the flu. That part is important because if she hadn't had the flu she would have gone out after work like the other nights, drinking too much and being in all the places that are supposed to be the wrong places at the wrong times. This night, she was home in her bed with the flu. He broke in, looking for his ex-girlfriend. Sarah was not his ex-girlfriend. She was a small statured 26-year-old lesbian who wanted to be a published author and who had moved to this city on a whim after growing tired of upstate New York and who just happened to be there. Wrong place. Wrong time. No one will ever know what was said. When the police finally found him a town over, he confessed right away

eiturlyf gjöld og grand lar-ceny, einn tilraun til morð ákæra sem hafði verið sleppt í ‹93. Hann hafði eytt nýjustu hrifningu sinni í fangelsi vegna gjalda sem tengjast heróíni og höfðu verið gefnar út fyrir viku síðan. Fyrrverandi kærasta hans vann með Söru á veitingastað og tveir höfðu búið saman í nokkrar vikur en Söru var á milli staða. Blaðið tilkynnti reikninga frá samstarfsfólki sínum að Hank myndi koma á veitingastaðnum flestum nætur, drukkinn, ógnandi að drepa fyrrverandi kærasta hans. Enginn tók hann mjög alvarlega, og kannski í nótt var ekki fyrsta nóttin sem hann braut inn í íbúðina en það var í fyrsta skipti sem einhver hafði verið þarna.

Hún hafði flensu. Sá hluti er mikilvægt vegna þess að ef hún hefði ekki haft flensu þá hefði hún farið út eftir vinnu eins og aðrar nætur, drukkið of mikið og verið á öllum stöðum sem eiga að vera rangar staðir á röngum tímum. Í nótt var hún heima í rúminu sínu með flensu. Hann braut inn og leit að fyrrverandi kærustu sinni. Sara var ekki fyrrverandi kærastan hans. Hún var lítill gömul 26 ára lesbía sem vildi vera skáldsaga höfundur og sem hafði flutt til þessa borgar á hegðun eftir að hafa verið þreyttur á New York-fylkinu og sem gerðist bara þarna. Rangt stað. Rangt tímabil. Enginn mun alltaf vita hvað var sagt. Þegar lögreglan loks fann hann bæinn yfir, játaði hann strax

gas y robo, y un atentado de homicidio que había sido dado de baja en 1993. Había pasado su última temporada en la cárcel por cargos relacionados con la heroína y había sido liberado hacía una semana. Su ex-novia trabajaba con Sarah en un restaurante y las dos habían estado viviendo juntas por un par de semanas mientras que Sarah estaba entre lugares. El periódico relató cuentas de sus compañeros de trabajo diciendo que Hank llegaba borracho al restaurante la mayoría de las noches, amenazando con matar a su ex-novia. Nadie lo tomaba muy en serio, y tal vez esta noche no era la primera vez que él irrumpió en el apartamento, pero fue la primera vez que alguien estaba allí.

Ella tenía la gripe. Esa parte es importante porque si ella no hubiera tenido la gripe ella hubiera salido después del trabajo como las otras noches, hubiera bebido demasiado e ido a todos los lugares que se supone que son el lugar equivocado en el momento equivocado. Esta noche, estaba en su cama con la gripe. Él entró a robar, o a matar, en busca de su ex-novia. Sarah no era su ex- novia. Ella era una lesbiana de pequeña estatura, de veintiséis años de edad que quería ser una autora publicada, y que se había cambiado a esta ciudad por capricho después de haberse cansado de la parte norte del estado de Nueva York y que se encontraba allí solo por casualidad. Lugar equivocado. Momento equivocado. Nadie sabrá nunca lo que fue dicho. Cuando la policía finalmente lo encontró un pueblo más adelante, confesó inmediatamente, diciendo que ella había

be za posjedovanje droge i teške krađe i jedna optužba za pokušaj ubojstva koja je povučena devedeset treće. Posljednje izdržavanje kazne zatvora bilo je je zbog optužbi o posjedovanju heroina, a otpušten je prije tjedan dana. Njegova je bivša djevojka radila sa Sarah u restoranu i njih su dvije privremeno živjele nekoliko tjedana zajedno dok si je Sarah tražila smještaj. Novine su izvijestile o kolegama s posla koje su rekle da je Hank uglavnom svake večeri znao svratiti u restoran, pijan, prijeteći da će ubiti svoju bivšu djevojku. Nitko ga nije shvaćao ozbiljno, i možda večeras nije prvi put da je provalio u stan, ali je prvi put da je netko bio ondje.

Imala je gripu. Taj je dio važan jer da nije bila imala gripu, bila bi izašla van nakon posla kao i svake noći, previše bi pila i nalazila se na pogrešnim mjestima u pogrešno vrijeme. Ove noći, ležala je u krevetu pod gripom. Provalio je u stan, tražeći svoju bivšu djevojku. Sarah nije bila njegova bivša djevojka. Bila je djevojka niska rasta, dvadesetšestogodišnjakinja, lezbejka koja je htjela postati objavljivani autor iznenada se preselivši u ovaj grad nakon što se zasitila „gornje države" New York – djevojka koja se samo zatekla ondje. Pogrešno mjesto. Pogrešno vrijeme. Nitko nikada neće znati što su si rekli. Kada ga je policija konačno pronašla u susjednom gradu, odmah je priznao ubojstvo kazavši da se ona prepirala s njim i isprovocirala njegov bijes.

saying that she had argued with him and provoked his rage.

Sarah wasn't much of an arguer, and even so, I can't imagine the sort of rage it takes to kill a person with a nail file and your fist. I can't imagine what brings a man to squeeze life from the neck of a stranger, in her bed with the flu. I can't imagine it. I won't imagine it. When I try, I can't tell how far away my toes are and my stomach folds over on itself. My body feels like an empty bag and I can't fill it.

This story happened three years ago, and now I'm one year older than she was when it happened and I am still so young. It happened before I understood the complexity of friendships between queer women and the way we can understand the subtleties in each other's stories. Before I knew how we hold onto each other and why and that things are rarely ever completely platonic. There were mornings I'd wake up in a bed at my parents house in a room which was not the one I grew up in and feel myself wishing she was there. I didn't know her well enough then to know what I was wishing for, but my body had already developed the innate understanding of a momentary urge to share intimacy with a person who understands your subtleties just by nature of understanding their own. In a way, I loved her. I was afraid of her a little bit because she lived so fully in her emotions and I hadn't learned how

að hún hefði haldið því fram við hann og valdið reiði sinni.

Söru var ekki mikið af rifrildi, og jafnvel þó að ég geti ekki ímyndað mér hvers konar reiði það tekur að drepa mann með nagli og hnefaleik. Ég get ekki ímyndað mér hvað veldur manni að kreista líf úr hálsi útlendinga, í rúminu sínu með flensu. Ég get ekki ímyndað mér það. Ég mun ekki ímynda mér það. Þegar ég reyni, get ég ekki sagt hve langt í burtu tærnar mínir eru og magurinn minn brýtur yfir sig. Líkami minn líður eins og tómt poka og ég get ekki fyllt það.

Þessi saga gerðist fyrir þremur árum, og nú er ég eitt ár eldri en hún var þegar það gerðist og ég er enn svo ungur. Það var áberandi áður en ég skildi hversu flókið vináttu var á milli annarra kvenna og hvernig við getum skilið næmi í sögum hvers annars. Áður en ég vissi hvernig við höldum á hvert annað og hvers vegna og það er sjaldan alltaf alveg platónískt. Það var morgnana að ég myndi vakna í rúminu í húsi foreldra míns í herbergi sem var ekki það sem ég ólst upp og fannst ég óska þess að hún væri þarna. Ég vissi hana ekki nógu vel til að vita hvað ég var að óska eftir, en líkaminn minn hafði albúið þróað meðfædda skilning á smávægilegri löngun til að deila nánd við manneskju sem skilur fíngerð þína bara í eðli sínu að skilja sjálfan sig. Á þann hátt elskaði ég hana. Ég var hræddur við hana svolítið vegna þess að hún lifði

discutido con él y que provocó su ira.

Sarah no era muy argumentista, y aún así, no me puedo imaginar la clase de ira que se necesita para matar a una persona con una lima de uñas y su puño. No me imagino lo que lleva a un hombre a exprimirle la vida desde el cuello a una extraña, en su cama, con la gripe. No puedo imaginarlo. Me niego a imaginarlo. Cuando lo intento, no sé cuán lejos están mis dedos de los pies y mi estómago se contrae sobre sí mismo. Mi cuerpo se siente como una bolsa vacía que no puedo llenar.

Esta historia sucedió hace tres años, y ahora tengo un año mas que ella cuando pasó y aun soy joven. Pasó antes de que yo comprendiera la complejidad de la amistad entre las mujeres "distintas" y la manera en la que podemos entender las sutilezas en las historias de cada una. Antes de saber cómo nos arraigamos mutuamente, y por qué, y que las cosas rara vez son totalmente platónicas. Hubo algunas mañanas en que desperté en cama, en casa de mis padres, en una habitación que no fue en la que yo crecí, y me sentía deseando que ella estuviera allí. No la conocía lo suficientemente bien entonces como para saber lo que estaba deseando, pero mi cuerpo ya había desarrollado la comprensión innata de un impulso momentáneo a compartir intimidad con una persona que entiende tus sutilezas sólo por la naturaleza de entender las suyas propias. En cierto modo, yo la amaba. Le tenía un poco de miedo porque ella vivía tan plenamente en sus emociones y yo no

Sarah nije bila neki tip svadljivice, čak i da je bila, ne mogu zamisliti vrstu bijesa koja je potrebna da ubiješ čovjeka šakom i turpijom za nokte. Ne mogu zamisliti što te može navesti da istisneš život iz vrata strancu, u vlastitom krevetu pod gripom. Ne mogu to zamisliti. Ne želim to zamisliti. Onda kada pokušavam, ne mogu procijeniti koliko su daleko moji nožni prsti dok se trbuh preklapa preko sebe samoga. Moje se tijelo osjeća poput prazne torbe koja se ne može napuniti.

Ova se priča dogodila prije tri godine, a sada sam godinu dana starija nego što je ona bila kada se to dogodilo, i još uvijek sam jako mlada. Dogodilo se prije nego sam uvidjela složenost prijateljstava između queer žena i načina na koji možemo razumjeti domišljatosti u međusobnim pričama. Prije nego sam znala kako se oslanjamo jedna na drugu i zašto i da su stvari rijetko kada u potpunosti platonske. Bilo je jutra kada bih se probudila u krevetu u kući svojih roditelja u sobi koja nije bila ona u kojoj sam odrastala i kada bih poželjela da je ona ovdje. Nisam je tada dovoljno dobro poznavala da bih znala što priželjkujem, ali moje je tijelo već razvilo prirođeno razumijevanje trenutačne težnje da podijeli prisnost s osobom koja razumije naše suptilnosti samo po prirodi razumijevanja svojih vlastitih. Na neki način, voljela sam ju. Pomalo sam je se bojala zato što je živjela tako potpuno u svojim osjećajima, a ja

to do that.

Now I think of her small bones, in a box in the cold earth by the old abandoned steel mill and our friends who raised the money for her tombstone because her parents couldn't afford it, and that's not the sort of thing you'd ever think to save up for in advance. I wrote her a poem and put it in a plastic bag and put the plastic bag in the tube in the ground that's meant to hold flowers. It has rained and snowed and rained and snowed and rained again and the paper is disintegrated but that bag is still there.

An empty bag where a poem used to be. Q

svo fullkomlega í tilfinningum hennar og ég hafði ekki lært hvernig á að gera það.

Nú hugsa ég um litla beinin hennar, í kassa í kulda jarðarinnar af gömlu yfirgefinum stálmylla og vinum okkar sem vakti peningana fyrir grafstein hennar vegna þess að foreldrar hennar gætu ekki fordæmt það og það er ekki það sem þú gerir Ég held alltaf að bjarga fyrirfram. Ég skrifaði henni ljóð og setti það í plastpoka og setti plastpokann í pípuna í jörðu sem ætlað er að halda blóm. Það hefur rignað og snowed og rigndi og snowed og rigndi aftur og pappír er sundur en þessi poki er enn þar.

Tómt poka þar sem ljóð var. Q

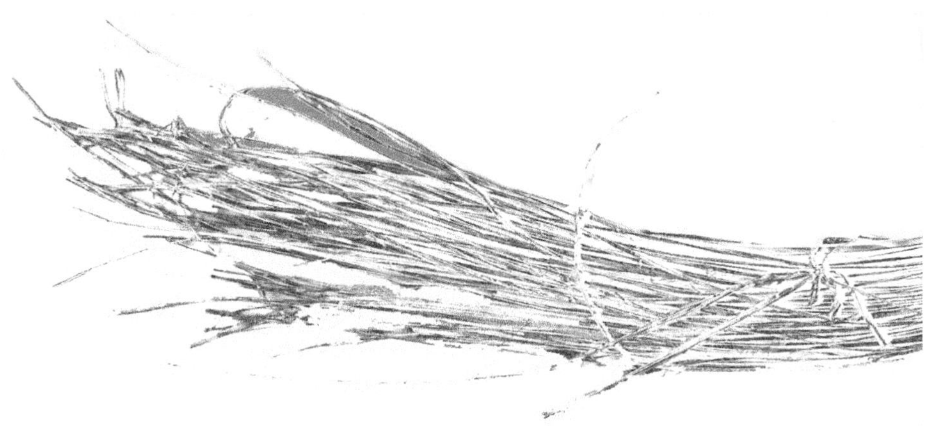

había aprendido a hacer eso.

Ahora pienso en sus pequeños huesos en una caja en la tierra fría cerca de la fábrica de acero abandonada, y en nuestros amigos que reunieron fondos para la lápida de su tumba, porque sus padres no podían pagarla, pues no es el tipo de cosa para la cual pensarías en ahorrar por adelantado. Le escribí un poema y lo puse en una bolsa de plástico y puse la bolsa en el tubo en la tierra que es para contener las flores. Ha llovido y nevado llovido y nevado y llovido otra vez y el papel se ha desintegrado, pero esa bolsa todavía está allí.

Una bolsa vacía donde antes había un poema. *Q*

nisam naučila kako to raditi.

Sada razmišljam o njezinim sitnim kostima, u lijesu u hladnoj zemlji pored stare napuštene čeličane i o našim prijateljima koji su prikupili novac za njezin nadgrobni spomenik jer ga njezini roditelji nisu mogli priuštiti, a to nije vrsta stvari za koju bi ikada pomislio da bi za nju trebalo unaprijed štedjeti. Napisala sam joj pjesmu i stavila je u plastičnu vrećicu koju sam stavila u cijev u zemlji koja je namjenjena da drži cvijeće. Kiši i snježi i kiši i snježi i kiši opet i papir je raspadnut, ali je vrećica još uvijek ondje.

Prazna vrećica u kojoj je pjesma znala biti. *Q*

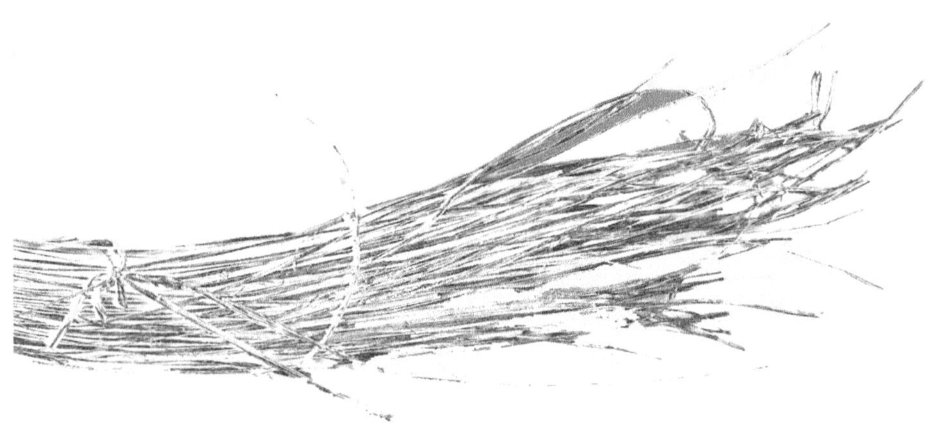

The Beguiling of Sofia Coppola: The architecture of the vacuum

Sergio Morera
(tr. fr. the Spanish, rvb)

The vacuum exists and is full —
Pascal

The Casimir effect

No doubt, it's cowardly to apologize in advance for the mistakes that can be made when giving an explanation. But it's naive to try to explain a theory about quantum physics and to think that one (who never opened a science book again after attaining the age of 17) will be able to do so satisfactorily. First of all, I apologize for what comes next.

The Casimir effect is a modern physics experiment that consists of placing two mirrors in a vacuum exactly the same, separated by a very small distance, and to show how these two bodies attract each other.

Contrary to what it may seem (and this is the experiment's grace), this approach doesn't occur because these bodies really attract each other, but it is due to the fact that they're constantly creating and destroying particles between these two mirrors in smaller amounts than those created and destroyed outside of the mirrors.

A seducción, de Sofia Coppola: La arquitectura del vacío

Sergio Morera

El vacío existe y está lleno
— Pascal

El efecto Casimir

Sin duda, es de cobardes disculparse por anticipado por los errores que se puedan cometer a la hora de dar una explicación. Pero es de ingenuos tratar de explicar una teoría relativa a la física cuántica y pensar que uno, que jamás volvió a abrir un libro de ciencias una vez cumplidos los 17 años, vaya a ser capaz de hacerlo de forma satisfactoria. Así pues, ante todo, pido perdón por lo que viene a continuación.

El efecto Casimir es un experimento de la física moderna que consiste en colocar en el vacío dos espejos exactamente iguales, separados por una distancia muy pequeña, y demostrar como estos dos cuerpos se atraen entre sí.

En contra de lo que pueda parecer (y ahí está la gracia del experimento) este acercamiento no se produce porque estos cuerpos se atraigan realmente entre sí, sino que se debe al hecho de que constantemente se están creando y destruyendo partículas entre estos dos espejos en menor cantidad que las que se crean y destruyen fuera de ellos.

„Opčinjen“ Sofije Coppole: Arhitektura vakuma

Sergio Morera

(prijevod, Ana Katana)

Vakum postoji i ispunjen je — Pascal

Casimirov efekt

Bez sumnje, kukavički je unaprijed se ispričavati za pogreške koje mogu nastati prilikom objašnjavanja. Unatoč tome, naivno je pokušavati objasniti neku teoriju o kvantnoj fizici i misliti da će netko (tko nije otvorio udžbenik iz prirodnih znanosti nakon navršenih sedamnaest godina) to uspješno učiniti. Stoga se prije svega ispričavam zbog onoga što slijedi.

Casimirov efekt je moderni fizički pokus koji se sastoji od stavljanja dvaju istovjetnih zrcala u vakum, te ih se sasvim malo razmakne, da bi se pokazalo kako se ta dva tijela međusobno privlače.

Suprotno od očekivanoga (u tome je ljepota pokusa), do toga ne dolazi zato što se ta dva tijela zaista međusobno privlače, nego zbog činjenice da ona neprestano stvaraju i uništavaju čestice između spomenuta dva zrcala u manjoj količini od onih koja se stvaraju i uništavaju izvan vakuma. Polje vanjskih čestica, koje je veće nego polje unutarnjih, gura ta dva tijela jedno prema drugome dok im se približava.

The field of outer particles, being greater than that of the interior, pushes these two bodies as it approaches them.

In short, what comes to reveal the Casimir effect is that the vacuum isn't "empty" as such, but has a structure of its own, with its own rules and laws, and that these are able to change the course of things.

It's a fascinating theory, not because of the complexity of the experiment itself, but because of its ability to reveal a whole hidden world where *a priori* there seemed to be absolutely nothing. Exactly the same thing that happens with Sofia Coppola's films and very especially in her latest work, *The Beguiled.*

The architecture of the vacuum

Emptiness. Sofia Coppola's work always revolves around this topic, but, while treated in a luminous manner in her previous films (a group of suicidal virgins lying on the grass, two strangers walking under Tokyo's neon, Marie Antoinette dancing among golden reflections in Versailles, a father and his daughter basking in the sun by a swimming

El campo de partículas exterior, al ser mayor que el del interior, empuja a estos dos cuerpos y los acerca.

En definitiva, lo que viene a desvelar el efecto Casimir es que el vacío no está "vacío" como tal, sino que posee una estructura propia, con sus propias normas y leyes, y que éstas son capaces de cambiar el rumbo de las cosas.

Esta en una teoría fascinante, no por la complejidad del experimento en sí, sino por su capacidad para revelar todo un mundo oculto allí donde a priori parecía no haber absolutamente nada. Exactamente lo mismo que sucede con el cine de Sofia Coppola y muy en especial en su último trabajo, *La seducción.*

La arquitectura del vacío

El vacío. La obra de Sofia Coppola siempre ha girado alrededor de este gran tema pero, mientras que en todos sus filmes anteriores este había sido tratado de forma luminosa (un grupo de Vírgenes Suicidas tendidas sobre la hierba, dos extraños paseando bajo los neones de Tokio, María Antonieta bailando entre reflejos dorados en Versalles, un padre y su hija

Ukratko, ono u čemu se naposljetku očituje Casimirov efekt jeste da vakum nije "prazan" kao takav, nego posjeduje vlastitu strukturu sa vlastitim zakonima i pravilima, koja pak imaju mogućnost promjene tijeka stvari.

Fascinantna je to teorija, ne samo zbog složenosti spomenutoga pokusa, nego i zbog njezine sposobnosti otkrivanja čitavog jednog skrivenog svijeta ondje gdje se *a priori* činilo da ne postoji apsolutno ništa. Upravo to se događa u filmovima Sofije Coppole, a posebice u njezinom posljednjem uratku, *Općinjen.*

Arhitektura vakuma

Praznina. Rad Sofije Coppole se uvijek vrti oko te teme, ali, dok se u njezinim ranijim filmovima praznina obavija blještavilom (skupina suicidalnih djevica leži na travi, dvoje stranaca šeće pod neonskim svjetlima Tokija, Marija Antoaneta pleše među zlatnim odsjajima Versaillesa, otac i kći lješkare na suncu po-

pool ...), *The Beguiled* reveals a surprising taste for darkness, structurally and formally.

Just as Junichiro Tanizaki's *In Praise of Shadows* tried to cure Western blindness by making us reflect on the importance of shadows in any artistic creation, Coppola seems determined with her new movie to draw our attention to the least known part of her work, that dark background that has always been present under the luminous surface of previous works.

The structure of the void is something that Sofia Coppola knows, and knows how to work perfectly, but in *The Beguiled* she seems to have wanted to explore it more in depth and make her particular Casimir experiment, using, as twin mirrors, another element that's served to define her work: spaces.

The confinement of Coppola's characters never occurs in just any place, architecture is of paramount importance in the films of the New York filmmaker because physical spaces always delimit the psychological spaces of the characters and are a reflection of these.

tomando el sol frente a una piscina...), *La seducción* sorprende en su gusto por la oscuridad, tanto argumental como formal.

De la misma forma que *El elogio de la sombra* de Junichiro Tanizaki trataba de curar la ceguera occidental haciéndonos reflexionar sobre la importancia de las sombras en toda creación artística, Coppola parece decidida con su nueva película a llamar nuestra atención sobre la parte menos conocida de su obra, ese reverso oscuro que siempre ha estado presente bajo la superficie luminosa de sus anteriores trabajos.

La estructura del vacío es algo que Sofia Coppola conoce y sabe trabajar a la perfección, pero en *La seducción* parece haber querido explorarla más en profundidad y hacer su particular experimento Casimir utilizando, a modo de espejos gemelos, otro de los elementos que le han servido para definir su obra: los espacios.

El confinamiento de los personajes de Coppola jamás se produce en un lugar cualquiera, la arquitectura es de suma importancia en las películas de la realizadora neoyorquina ya que los espacios físicos delimitan siempre los espacios psicológicos de los personajes y constituyen un reflejo de éstos.

red bazena...), *Opčinjen* otkriva iznenađujuću sklonost ka mraku, i strukturalno i formalno gledano.

Baš kao što je *In Praise of Shadows* Junichira Tanizakija pokušao izliječiti zapadnjačko sljepilo tjerajući nas da razmislimo o važnosti sjena u svim umjetničkim tvorevinama, Coppola je svojim novim uratkom odlučila privući našu pozornost na onaj nepoznati dio svoga stvaralaštva, onu mračnu pozadinu koja je uvijek bila prisutna ispod bliještavih površina.

Struktura praznine je Coppolino područje, i savršeno je iskorištava, ali u *Opčinjenome* se čini da ju je željela istražiti još dublje, izvršiti vlastiti Casimirov pokus, a umjesto istovjetnih zrcala, koristila se drugim elementom kojim se definira njezino stvaralaštvo: prostorima. Zatočenost Coppolinih likova nikada nije slučajna. Arhitektura predstavlja krucijalni element u uratcima njujorške filmašice zato što materijalni prostori uvijek ograničavaju psihološke prostore likova i predstavljaju njihov odraz.

The vacuum in *Marie-Antoinette* is reflected in the windows and tapestries of Versailles, the disenchanted protagonist of *Somewhere* on the walls of the Chateau Marmont, *The Bling Ring*'s young burglars in the minimalist Los Angeles mansions and, as it could not be any other way, the girls and women of Miss Farnsworth's school for young ladies is reflected in the Madewood Plantation House in Louisiana.

This is perhaps the film in which you can see Coppola more radically use this relationship of subject to space, the old mansion's levels arranged as kinds of walls around the action and the characters. At the start of each sequence we invariably find those same images, barely distinguishable, of the Madewood Plantation House; its columns, its top row of balconies, the veranda, the orchard.

As the film progresses, thanks to this firm narrative structure based on repetition, we perceive something that wasn't appreciated in the director's other films, and that is precisely the pressure of the external as it threatens to make the internal disapppear, made famous by the Casimir effect. The weight of history (columns of smoke behind the trees and the sound of bombs on one side and the slow advance of the vegetation planted by the slaves on the other) will close little by little on this white mansion, and it will inevitably come to be that there, where once there was something (dreams, hopes) the mysterious architecture of the vacuum will rule again. *Q*

El vacío de *María Antonieta* se refleja en las cristaleras y tapices de Versalles, el del desencantado protagonista de *Somewhere* en las paredes del Chateau Marmont, el de los jóvenes ladrones de *The Bling Ring* en las minimalistas mansiones de Los Angeles y, como no podía ser de otra manera, el de las niñas y mujeres de la Escuela Para Señoritas Farnsworth se refleja en la Madewood Plantation House de Louisiana.

Esta es quizá la película en la que se puede apreciar un uso más radical de Coppola en esta relación del sujeto con su espacio ya que los planos de esta vieja mansión están dispuestos como una especie de muralla alrededor de la acción y los personajes. En el inicio de cada secuencia nos vamos a encontrar invariablemente con esas mismas imágenes, apenas indiferenciables, de la Madewood Plantation House; sus columnas, su balconada superior, el porche, el huerto.

A medida que avanza el filme, gracias a esta firme estructura narrativa basada en la repetición, percibimos algo que no se apreciaba en el resto de películas de la directora y que es, precisamente, esa presión de lo externo que amenaza con hacer desaparecer lo interno que hizo célebre al efecto Casimir.

El peso de la historia (las columnas de humo tras los árboles y el sonido de las bombas por un lado y el lento avance de la vegetación plantada por los esclavos por otro) se irá cerrando poco a poco sobre esta blanca mansión y hará que allí donde alguna vez hubo algo (sueños, esperanzas) vuelva a reinar de nuevo la misteriosa arquitectura del vacío. *Q*

The Construction of the Kraftwerk Concentration Camp at Lužniki Stadium

they looked at us from the stage
the way naked men look into the eyes
of naked women

none of us turned our gaze

⁕

they could have done anything they wanted with us

that is probably how my grandfather felt in 1945
driving his tank
along the small brittle streets
his strength made him shy
he was afraid the German girls would laugh at him

⁕

the fingers of Ralf Hütter moved
like Jewish girls
performing in that circus
where they sadly walk
along barbed wire
beneath the camp cupola

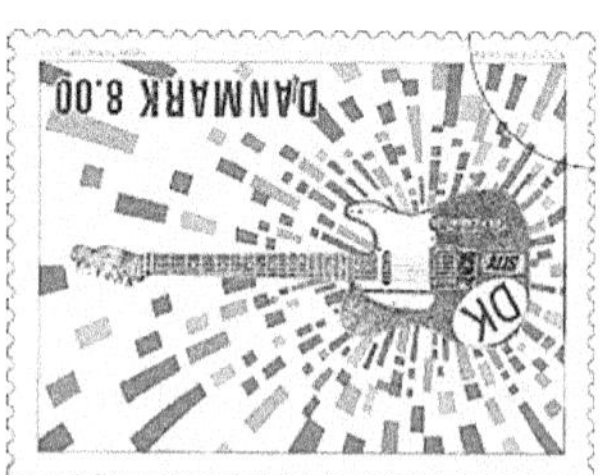

⁕

all night I dreamed of the
Tour de France
for which they wrote the soundtrack
commemorating the centennial
they were to first to understand
that through the broken lenses of glass bicycles
France's most hidden government secret is revealed

— *Andrei Sen-Senkov*
(tr. fr. the Russian, Ainsley Morse & Peter Golub)

La construcción del campo de concentración de Kraftwerk en el Estadio Lužniki

nos miraban desde la tarima
en la misma forma en que los hombres desnudos miran a los ojos
de las mujeres desnudas

ninguno de nosotros bajó nuestra mirada

✯

podrían haber hecho lo que querían con nosotros

que es probablemente cómo mi abuelo sentía en 1945
conduciendo su tanque
por las pequeñas y frágiles calles
su fuerza lo hacía tímido
le tenía miedo a las muchachas alemanas se reirían de él

✯

los dedos de Ralf Hütter se movían
como chicas judías
actuando en ese circo
donde tristemente caminan
a lo largo de alambre de púas
bajo la cúpula del campo

toda la noche soñé con el
Tour de Francia
para el que se escribió la banda sonora
para conmemorar el centenario
fueron los primeros en entender
que a través de los lentes rotos de bicicletas de cristal
el secreto más oculto del gobierno de Francia es revelado

— *Andrei Sen-Senkov*
(traducción, T. Warburton y Bajo y rvb)

Izgradnja Kraftwerkova koncentracijskog logora na stadionu Lužnjiki

gledali su nas s pozornice
kao što goli muškarci zure u oči
golih žena

ni jedno među nama nije svrnulo pogled

✸

mogli su nam učiniti što su htjeli

tako se vjerojatno mmoj djed osjećao 1945.
dok je vozio svoj tenk
malenim i krhkim ulicama
srameći se svoje snage
bojao se da će mu se Njemice smijati

✸

prsti Ralfa Hűttera pomicali su se
poput židovskih djevojaka
dok nastupaju u onom cirkusu
kada tužno koračaju
uz bodljikavu žicu
pod logorskom kupolom

✸

cijelu sam noć sanjao
Tour de France [1]
za koji sam napisao popis pjesama
obilježavajući stogodišnjicu
prvi su shvatili da se kroz slomljene leće staklenih bicikala
otkriva najskrivenija tajna francuske vlade

— *Andrei Sen-Senkov*
(prijevod, Jelena Pataki)

[1] Tour de France naziv je albuma njemačke glazbene skupine Kraftwerk

НЕ ПИШИТЕ ПИСЬМА. ИХ ПОТОМ ЧИТАЮТ

в одном из писем
чехов долго рассказывает
как накануне он освобождал мышей
попавших в мышеловку

отпуская их
он записывал на видеокамеру карандаша
литературную формулу-1
серых маленьких машинок
с живыми дверцами
открывающимися в кровь

а все его знаменитые чеховские рассказы
написаны так же случайно
как случайно

записывают куски телепередач на кассету с
любимым фильмом

— Андрей Сен-Сеньков

Don't Write Letters. They Are Read Afterwards

in one of his letters
Chekhov divulged at length
how the day before he released mice
stuck in the mousetrap

releasing them
he recorded on the video camera of his pencil
the literary Formula One
small grey cars
with living doors
that open into blood

and all of his famous Chekhovian stories
were recorded just as fortuitously
as when
people recorded pieces of miscellaneous shows
onto the cassette with their favorite movie

— Andrei Sen-Sekov
(tr. fr. the Russian, Ainsley Morse & Peter Golub)

No escriba cartas. Son leídos después

en una de sus cartas
Chejov divulgó con mucho detalle
cómo el día anterior soltó ratones
atrapados en la ratonera

liberándolos
grabó en la cámara de vídeo de su lápiz
la obra literaria Fórmula Uno
pequeños coches grises
con puertas vivas
que se abren en sangre

y todos sus famosas historias Chejovianas
se grabaron fortuitamente
como cuando
la gente graba fragmentos de diversos espectáculos
en el casete con su película favorita

— Andrei Sen-Sekov
(traducción, T. Warburton y Bajo y rvb)

Nemojte pisati pisma. Ona se čitaju kasnije

u jednom je od svojih pisama
Čehov razotkrio u mnoštvo detalja
kako je prethodnog dana oslobodio miševe
zarobljene u mišolovci

oslobađajući ih
snimio je kamerom svoje olovke
književnu Formulu Jedan
male sive automobile
sa živim vratima
koja se otvaraju u krv

i sve njegove poznate Čehovljeve priče
su zabilježene baš tako slučajno
kao i kada
su ljudi presnimili dijelove različitih emisija
na kasetu s njihovim omiljenim filmom.

— Andrei Sen-Senkov
(prijevod, Dijana Jakovac)

Knut Van Brijs,
Iconic/ikonische/икона, bricolage (2017)